Always Inspired

# Always Inspired
## Why Bible-Believing Christians
## Need the Catholic Church

**Basil Christopher Butler**
Abbot of Downside

Sophia Institute Press
Manchester, NH

*Always Inspired* was first published under the title
*The Church and the Bible* by Darton, Longman, & Todd, Ltd.,
London: 1960. © Basil Christopher Butler 1960, 2012.

Sophia Institute Press
Box 5284, Manchester, NH 03108
1-800-888-9344
www.SophiaInstitute.com
Sophia Institute Press® is a registered trademark of Sophia Institute.

Cover design by Carolyn McKinney.

Photo credit: Council of Nicaea, Novogrod School,
Gianni Dagli Orti / The Art Archive at Art Resource, NY

Printed in the United States of America.

*Nihil Obstat:* Joannes M. T. Barton, STD LSS. *Censor Deputatis.*
*Imprimatur:* E. Morrogh Bernard, *Vicar General.*
Westmonasterii, die 31A Januarii, 1959.

**Library of Congress Cataloging-in-Publication Data**

Butler, Basil Christopher.
 [Church and the Bible]
 Always inspired : why Bible-believing Christians need the Catholic Church /
B.C. Butler.
    p. cm.
 Originally published: The church and the Bible. London : Darton, Longman
& Todd, 1960.
 "An ARKive edition."
 Includes bibliographical references and index.
 ISBN 978-1-933184-79-1 (ppbk : alk. paper)
1. Bible—Study and teaching—Catholic Church. 2. Catholic Church—
Doctrines. I. Title.
 BS587.B85 2012
 220.6088'282—dc22

                    2010029528

# Contents

*NOTE*

*The three chapters of this book originally formed the three
Lauriston Lectures for 1958 and the informal style of the spoken
word has been retained.*

# CHAPTER ONE

# A View from Outside

WE BELIEVE that Our Lord gave to his Church a mission to all men in all places and for all historical time: 'You must go out, making disciples of all nations, and baptizing them in the name of the Father and of the Son and of the Holy Ghost, teaching them to observe all the commandments which I have given you. And behold I am with you all through the days that are coming, until the consummation of the world' (Mt. 28: 19f.).

It is part of good missionary technique to try to enter into the point of view of those you are trying to convert; to see yourself and your message, for a moment, as they see you and it. So doing you can hope to remove their misconceptions, and not to drive them still further from the truth by the use of language and of an approach which they will inevitably misconstrue.

So let us ask ourselves how an intelligent unbeliever would view the Christian fact in history. He would see Christianity as one of the great world faiths, alongside Islam, Hinduism, Buddhism, Confucianism and Taoism.

And he might reflect that at the present day it is numerically the largest, probably, of these conglomerations of believers.[1]

How is Christianity distinguished from the other great faiths? To begin with, it might be pointed out that Judaism (which though not numerically great is very widespread), Islam and Christianity form a single group of religions, whose peculiarity is that these three all claim to rest their teaching on truth historically revealed by God, not merely on human reflection and discovery. This revelation, they claim, was given by God at particular moments or periods to individuals or groups entrusted with the task of passing on the truth thus revealed to others. We owe the steam engine to the intelligence and inventiveness of a particular man, but in theory it was open to anyone, who was clever enough, to harness steam to human use; whereas a prophet is one who is entirely dependent for his message on God who chooses to reveal it to him. In contrast to this idea of divine revelation, the Buddha, for instance, is represented as an earnest thinker who, as the result of long strife of soul, discovered for himself a truth or mode of life which he then, in the kindness of his heart, wished to share with others, so that they in their turn might enjoy the emancipation which it had brought him. Similarly, neither

[1] 'Of the . . . human beings on earth, nearly 800 million—one out of every three—are listed as Christians' (Paul Hitchinson, *Life*, 6 February 1956).

Confucius nor Lao-tse, the founder of Taoism, claimed, so far as we can judge, to be more than a wise man passing on, doubtless with improvements due to himself, the traditional wisdom of past ages. Hinduism points to many 'saviours', but on examination they seem to have been religious geniuses or holy men who had by their piety and goodness made themselves as it were translucent to that spiritual truth which is available, on the Indian view, to all who seek it, without any special divine intervention or revelation.

Thus it is a distinguishing feature of Judaism, Christianity and Islam, as compared with these other great faiths, that they claim to possess and to hand on a divine revelation—indeed, up to a point, they all transmit the same revelation. The roots of Christianity are in the faith, the practice, and the tradition of ancient Israel, to which of course modern Judaism also looks back; and Christianity has refused to disown its Israelite or Jewish past.[1] Islam, from the point of view of the impartial unbeliever, could be described as something like a heresy or aberration from the main stream of Israelite-Christian orthodoxy; it recognizes the authority of the Israelite prophets, and even views Jesus Christ as one of the greatest prophets. But for Islam, and here of course Judaism and Christianity disagree with it, the supreme

[1] In the second century A.D. a Christian named Marcion argued that the 'God' of the Old Testament was not the Father of Jesus Christ. But this idea was rejected by the Church, and Marcion is regarded as a heretic.

prophet is Mahomet, and the revelation which he received is deposited in the Koran.

The notion of revelation, of the revealed 'word' of God to man, puts these three faiths together over against the other great world-faiths.[1] It means, for those who accept it, that man has not been left to his own unaided resources in the search for a truth by which he may live and in the strength of which he may have hope, but that God the creator and judge of all men has, in his limitless mercy, put out a hand to help us in our gropings towards him (Acts 17 : 27); has told us what we need to know about himself and his will. Christianity adds that this divine self-revelation was made in an act of redeeming love; not truth only but grace has come to us through Jesus Christ.

Christianity, in fact, has taken this notion of revela-

---

[1] The idea of revelation is by no means confined to these three faiths. It was common in antiquity, for instance in the rather degraded form of belief in oracles. Plato (*Phaedo*, 85d) makes one of his characters suggest, rather wistfully, that a 'divine word', were it available, would be a trusty vessel for the voyage of life. Lucretius, the great Latin poet who expounded in verse the anti-religious materialism of Epicurus, allows himself, in a poetic exordium, to write of his revered master: 'If our speech is to match the sublimity of his teaching, a god was he who first discovered that explanation of life which is now called Philosophy, and who by his skill rescued life from such storms and darkness and established it in such tranquillity and brilliant light' (V, 7–12). But it will be observed that it is the presumed truth of Epicurus's teaching which leads Lucretius to speak of it as though it were revelation. For the religious believer, it is the presumed authenticity of a revelation which leads him to accept its content as true. The philosopher has inverted the order of faith.

tion, of a word of God revealed by God himself to man, and has pushed it to its furthest limits—has developed the notion, so to speak, to its perfect stature. Judaism and Christianity both teach that God uttered his word through Moses and the prophets of Israel, and so 'spoke' to the Old Testament People of God 'through the prophets' (Heb. 1: 1), who were purely human mediators or transmitters of the divine message. But the Christian adds that 'in these last days' he has spoken a final and complete word to man in Jesus Christ his Son (ibid., 1: 2): 'The word' of God 'was made flesh and came to dwell among us' (Jn. 1: 14). Here there is no distinction between the word and its human mediator; the human Jesus is the word which he transmits. The Man Jesus Christ, to whom we look back as the founder of our faith and the source of our saving knowledge of God, was in his own person, as involved in his historical life and death and in his resurrection, both the revealer of truth and the truth revealed; he was 'the word who was originally with God and was himself God', and in becoming man he did not cease to be what he eternally was. Nor is he just *a* word of God; he is *the* word, 'in whom the whole treasury of wisdom and knowledge is stored up' (Col. 2: 3). All previous revelation was summed up and re-expressed in him, and no further disclosure of divine truth, beyond that which may be found in him, may be looked for by the believer.[1]

[1] 'He that would now enquire of God, or seek any vision or revela-

The word of God made man, Jesus Christ, did not come to a world entirely unprepared to receive him. As has been said, the Christian Church affirms the truth for its own age of the Old Testament revelation. It is thus part of the Christian message that God had been educating the People of Israel for centuries to a knowledge of himself and his will higher and more effective than that to which other peoples had attained. God had not left mankind without any evidence of his provident care in those ages preceding the incarnation of his Son. Creation itself is attributed, in Ps. 32: 6, and in Gen. 1: 3, to a word of God: 'God said, Let there be light; and there was light. . . .' So the created universe, which exists only in obedience to God's word and according to the content of that word, is in some sense a reflection of the thought of God expressed therein. 'God's eternal power and divineness', says St. Paul, are understood and made manifest in the things which he has made (Rom. 1: 20). But on the basis of what we may call the general revelation of the created order there has also

tion, would not only be acting foolishly, but would be committing an offence against God by not setting his eyes altogether upon Christ, and seeking no new thing or aught besides. And God might answer him after this fashion, saying: If I have spoken all things to thee in my Word, which is my Son, and I have no other word, what answer can I now make to thee, or what can I reveal to thee which is greater than this? Set thine eyes on him alone, for in him I have spoken and revealed to thee all things, and in him thou shalt find yet more than that which thou asked and desirest' (St. John of the Cross, *Ascent of Mount Carmel*, II, xxii, 5, tr. Allison Peers).

been a system of progressive special revelation to Israel, above all in the days of Moses and of the establishment of the 'covenant' between Israel and God at that time.

I have described as a divine education of Israel this long process of revelation leading up to the final incarnation of the word of God, itself a further revelation which recapitulated all that had gone before. As in the education of an individual, each new stage in such a process of national education builds upon the enlightenment previously given in earlier stages. In the case of an individual child or man, education depends upon his possession of the faculty of memory. Of course he needs intelligence as well as memory, but intelligence by itself is not enough. It is in the memory that past lessons are stored up and lie ready to serve as the basis for subsequent more advanced lessons. Without memory or the capacity to acquire bodily skills and habits, we should be incapable of being educated; in fact, we should be unable to cope with life at all. Sometimes owing to an accident a man suffers a partial 'loss of memory'. Supposing that at the age of thirty someone loses the memory of all that he has experienced and learnt since the age of fifteen, he will have to be re-educated from that point; otherwise he will not be adjusted to a world which has gone on progressing for fifteen years of which he appears to have no knowledge.

Memory, then, is what makes an individual capable of learning, capable of being educated, provided that he has at least the glimmerings of intelligence. What is it in society, in a nation for instance like ancient Israel, which corresponds to memory in the single individual? It is something that I want to be allowed to call tradition. By tradition I mean the passing on, by whatever means may be employed, of the fruits of experience and education from one generation to its successors. The word tradition means, etymologically, handing over or handing on. I shall use it to mean both the process of handing on and the contents of what is thus handed on. It may be a truth or an alleged truth that is handed on (as, for instance, a legend of a family ghost in an ancestral home), or it may be a mode of behaviour—such, for instance, as the tradition in a certain school that one makes the sign of the cross on passing a particular statue of Our Lady (I am told that this goes back to a period when the Blessed Sacrament was reserved in a spot behind where the statue stands).

Tradition is stored up and transmitted in a variety of ways. Raising your hat to a lady is a traditional gesture of courtesy, which boys learn both from the behaviour of those about them and from actual teaching given to them by their elders; in another area of culture—that is to say, in a different stream of tradition—a similar meaning of reverence is attached to the act of removing your shoes: 'Put off thy shoes from thy feet, for the place whereon thou standest is holy ground' (Exod. 3: 5). Then again there are traditions of craftsmanship. The things made by one generation, pots or pans or houses or weapons or pictures, convey a lesson of skill and an insight upon which the next generation may improve; so we get the evolution of styles of architecture from Romanesque to Perpendicular. Language itself is a crystallization of experience and a set of audible signs, a tradition, and an immensely valuable one, because it becomes a vehicle of tradition, a means by which so much information can be rapidly transmitted which would otherwise not be passed on at all, or only very slowly and clumsily—as we realize when we travel in a country where we do not understand the language of the natives. Rites and ceremonies, manners, and the customs of the tribe or nation, are all parts of tradition; they all fulfil a function of education, which of course is something far wider than schooling. And along with all these traditional elements there goes, conveyed by the great tradition of language, oral tradition in song and folklore and legend, binding each new generation to the past of the nation, teaching it the wisdom of the ages, and giving it a directive for its further advance and a framework for the new contribution which, in its turn, it will make to this inherited store and hand on, with it, to the future. Tradition, in short, is much the same as culture; it is something that makes the life of man in society something other than the nasty, short, brutish and intolerable thing of which Hobbes wrote.

It is obvious that tradition can have a bad influence.

It can stifle and kill initiative, just as in the life of the individual the memory of his own past can weigh a man down like a burden from which he would gladly shake himself free. And as an individual may have bad habits, so a society can have corrupt traditions. But without tradition progress is impossible. Philosophy, the sciences, and the arts all have their traditions; so have schools and universities, villages, cities and countrysides and nations. So too have religious bodies—even those that profess the strongest dislike for the idea of tradition. The individual or group that revolts from tradition does so, often enough, on the basis of what he has learnt from tradition. Thus it was in the name of the Bible, a traditional loyalty learnt from the Catholic Church, that early Protestants opposed Catholicism. Tradition in fact, as we said, is to society what memory is to the individual; it may be called corporate memory, or the inherited contents of the mind of society. A loss of tradition, total or partial, is for any society, for tribe or nation or religious communion, what loss of memory is for the individual; so far as it occurs, to that extent the society in question has to begin at the beginning again.

This close association of society and tradition is especially to be observed by us, because the Christian revelation, God's word to man, was not a private revelation made separately to separate individuals, but a public revelation made to a particular human group, though intended, Christianity declares, for all mankind. Such a revelation, made at a particular place and time, and therefore given immediately to only a particular local group living then and there, can obviously only be a revelation for others at other places and at subsequent times if it is transmitted to them by some process which, unless it is telepathic, will fall under the heading of what we are here calling tradition. Our link with the historical Jesus is a traditional link. We note in passing the problem of assuring that the content of the revelation, its whole truth and nothing but its truth, is conveyed pure and total to those who have no direct means of checking what they receive by tradition. But especially we note that this business of tradition, of handing on the revelation, implies all along the social character of our human lot. Christianity has no room for pure individualism; it is excluded by the nature of the central Christian claim that God spoke to all men by and in a particular historical life. We may even be predisposed to expect that the supreme revelation, in the Word of God incarnate, entrusted to a guaranteed process of transmission, will have been made in connection with the notion of corporateness pushed to its furthest point in a fully fledged autonomous society. In any case, we see already the close association of the three notions: public revelation, tradition, and man's social nature.

So far we have said nothing of one of the most powerful and important of all vehicles of tradition, one that belongs specially to the subject of the Church and the

Bible: the art of writing. We do not know at what date writing was invented, but we know that it goes back to about 3000 B.C. However early we choose to place it, it must be presumed to have been a comparatively late invention, at least in the developed form in which it became useful for the preserving of comprehensive records. In itself, of course, it is merely a set of systematic conventional signs, a development from such devices as the blazing of trees; and who knows how early man may have begun to employ such mnemonic devices? The elaboration of writing as a means of communication on a large scale will have been a slow process, and one of those in which early rudimentary success may have proved an obstacle to some further advances. Those who have followed the fortunes of Bernard Shaw's attempt to provide for a simplification of English spelling will have had a contemporary illustration of the way in which past achievement blocks the way for change.

Two important points must be borne in mind in connection with the invention and the history of the art of writing. In the first place, writing early became a skill possessed by a special and very limited class, to whom it gave both power and prestige. It has been quite unusual for a whole adult population, like that of the Anglo-Saxon countries today, to be almost entirely literate. Secondly, writing and written records never completely absorb or supersede the other vehicles of tradition; these continue to play their part, perhaps a somewhat reduced part, in the education of succeeding generations, in the transmission of culture—including, naturally, religious education or culture. Even today oral lectures have their place in the educational system of our universities. This survival of non-literary vehicles or elements of tradition is inevitable, both because society always has its quota of illiterates (children, for instance) who have to receive their 'education' through other channels than their own reading; and also because the written word, in the normal case, never succeeds in embodying more than a fraction of the total constituents of a culture or a tradition. Anyone who has lived in country places and learnt to understand and love them knows that the traditional culture of the countryside is something far wider, far richer, far more intangible, than all that can be set down in writing of it. It lives in song and dance and drama, in dialect and intonation and idiom, in tales told in the nursery and by the winter fireside; in gesture and local technique and craft and custom. It is like an inspiration reborn from generation to generation, like the 'light of Christ' of the Paschal Vigil, passed on from one bearer to another till the original source, maybe, is lost sight of, though the splendour does not fade. Too often, the spread of literacy, which brings so many blessings in its train, acts like an antibiotic on this genuine and humane tradition. And is it not a matter of common observation that an unwritten constitution is in many respects a happier and a healthier thing than one that states itself exhaustively in a written document?

The books of the Old Testament are, for the historian, a collection of documents illustrating the developing religious tradition of pre-Christian Israel. They are the survivors of a body of literature which, if it had all been preserved, would doubtless have been very extensive. They include books which are usually classed as historical (for instance, the Books of Kings) and along with them collections of prophecies, psalms (that is, religious hymns), and books of proverbial or traditional 'wisdom'. The Jews (whose list of canonical books is rather less extensive than that of our Old Testament) divided this official scripture into three departments: the Law (Torah, that is the five 'books of Moses'), the Prophets (which included, be it noted, the four Books of Kings or of the Kingdoms), and the Writings (Psalms, Proverbs, etc.). To the Jews of the period immediately preceding the Christian era the most important part of this collection of books was, as it remains today, the Pentateuch, or five 'books of Moses': Genesis, Exodus, Leviticus, Numbers and Deuteronomy. The Pentateuch was sometimes referred to as the Law of Moses. This Law or (as we might better translate *torah*), this record of revelation viewed as a guide to right living, had by the beginning of our era become the governing basis of Jewish faith and practice; to such an extent that there was a tendency to regard the revelations of the prophets later than Moses as not adding to, but only partially restating and perhaps expounding, the revelation once given through Moses at Sinai. Most of the Old Testament books are written in Hebrew, the ancestral language of the Israelites, but Aramaic (which had by Our Lord's time largely superseded Hebrew as the spoken language of the Jews) appears in some of the later strata of the Old Testament, and some books were originally written in Greek, or have survived only in Greek translation and in translations from the Greek.

For over a century critical scholarship has been hard at work on the Old Testament books. Broadly speaking, these books reveal to modern scholarship the story of the early and protracted struggles and the eventual triumph in Israel of faith in Jahveh, the Lord, affirmed in at least the later strata of the literature as the one holy creator, who, it was believed, had chosen Israel for his peculiar people, had made his 'covenant' with them, had watched over and intervened in their long national history, rewarding their corporate obedience and punishing their collective sins; and who would one day intervene again to establish among them, and perhaps through them over all mankind, his perfect reign or 'kingdom'. These documents also show, in their latest strata, a deepened and positive interest in the life after death. As we know from the Gospels, even in Our Lord's day the Sadducean wing of Palestinian Judaism rejected the Pharisaic view that there would be a bodily resurrection for the righteous; this need not mean that they rejected all idea of an after-life. Naturally, as this positive interest in a life beyond the grave developed, it was held that the quality of the after-life would be determined by the moral and religious quality of the life lived on earth, which thus tended to be regarded at a time of probation.

I have described the books of the Old Testament, as they are seen by an independent historian (and so far we are not taking account of what the teaching of the Church has to tell us about their inspiration) as 'illustrative documents'. They open windows for us with tantalizing glimpses of a long story of Israelite culture and religious history. By themselves, they raise for the historian more problems than they solve. Modern research, archaeology, and general historical investigation have thrown a flood of new light upon them, and upon the tradition of national life and corporate religious faith and practice which lie behind them, and from which they spring.

It is true that the Judaism of immediately pre-Christian times was already to a large extent, as Judaism is today, the religion of a 'book' (really, as we have seen, of a collection of books). It was a religion which, in default of any recognized contemporary public prophecy, looked to this 'book' as its ultimate available authority; the appeal to Scripture could only be met by offering an alternative interpretation of the texts appealed to. But in fact the national religious tradition was not only dependent on, not exclusively enshrined in, this literature. It had a second focus in the Temple of Jerusalem and in the hereditary priesthood and the sacrificial system of the Temple. Palestine itself was for the Jews a Holy Land. And the Law, meaning by that the Mosaic code as contained in the Pentateuch, was not treated, at least by the more advanced religious party, the Pharisees, as sufficient to itself, whatever their theories may have been. On the contrary, as was inevitable, the written code of laws was found, in the course of centuries, to need interpretation and amplification and qualification in its application to changed and often unforeseen circumstances. The historian will see the signs of such historical development in the actual Mosaic code itself as it stands in the Old Testament; many of its detailed prescriptions, he will tell us, come from dates long subsequent to Moses himself.[1] The tradition of God's actual revelation of himself and his will through Moses and the prophets remained the

[1] Just as 'David' stands for the authorship of sacred psalms, and 'Solomon' for the wisdom of the Jewish sages, so 'Moses', it might be suggested, stands for the legislative authority. I am not of course suggesting that Moses himself was not in fact a law-giver. And it may be well to repeat that we are here stating the case as it appears in the light of historical science today, without reference to the Church's teaching about the Bible. Historical science is fallible and has its temporary fashions, like natural science.

guiding principle of Jewish faith and practice; but it
acted upon the conscience of the contemporaries of Our
Lord within the context and framework of a wider
tradition, and in a form which was in some ways or
parts more developed than it had had in primitive days
—only so was it an operative and living factor in the
national and religious life of the people, and in the life
of the individual Jews. Once again we see that, while
tradition is a necessary corollary to the idea of a public
revelation made at particular times and places but intended for a wider audience, so too on the other hand
the transmission of revelation by tradition presupposes
the social life of the community or culture for which it
is intended. Revelation, man's social nature tending to
actual life in a society, and tradition—once more we are
back with these three interrelated realities.

Indeed the very basis of Judaism was the fact and the
idea of the Chosen People of God. God, for the Jews,
was not the conclusion of a philosophic argument; he
was Jahveh, the Lord, who had wonderfully visited and
redeemed his people (above all in the Exodus and at
Sinai), of which people he was the spiritual bond. In the
history of Israel they found the evidence of God's power
and providence and character; he was not the 'sort of
God' who might work miracles and show mercy; he
was the God who had miraculously rescued, mercifully
forgiven, and wisely guided his actual historical people
—and who could therefore be expected to act again in

the future, on the 'day' of his choice and predestination, for the redemption of that same people. 'You only have I known, of all the families of the earth' (Amos 3: 2; the word 'know' here means an intimate knowledge coinciding with preferential choice—it does not mean that God was unconscious of the rest of mankind, but that, compared with Israel, he ignored them). This was the conviction, at once elevating and humbling, by which the faithful Israelite lived; this the vision in which he saw the whole of his personal and national life, the whole fact and story and prospects of God's universe. When he looked for further blessings from God in the hoped-for future, he automatically thought of these as destined for the people as a whole, though perhaps a people purified by the extrusion of impious elements.[1] Divine blessing would come to the individual only as a member of the people or as in some way related to it. The Jew did not normally think of religious truth as an abstract system of 'orthodoxy' independent of all social embodiment; for him the truth was bound up with the life of the People of God.

It was to this Chosen People of God that the ministry

[1] 'We are introduced by the Dead Sea Scrolls to a group of people who believed that they constituted the true and ideal Congregation of Israel, the small remnant that had stayed faithful to the traditional Covenant and that was thereby ensuring the continuance of God's people and the eventual cleansing of his land from the stain of guilt' (T. H. Gaster, *The Scriptures of the Dead Sea Sect in English Translation* Secker & Warburg, 1957, p. 13).

of Jesus was addressed: 'I am not sent save to the lost sheep of the house of Israel' (Mt. 15: 24); 'Do not think that I have come to set aside the law and the prophets', i.e. the bases of Old Testament faith and practice; 'I have not come to set them aside, but to bring them to perfection' (Mt. 5: 17). He claimed to be proclaiming and introducing the 'reign of God' which was the hope of Israel (the 'kingdom of heaven' in our versions of the Bible represents an Aramaic or Hebrew phrase better translated 'reign of God'): 'There have been many prophets and just men who have longed to see what you see, to hear what you hear, and never heard it' (Mt. 13: 17). When two of John the Baptist's followers came with the question: 'Is it thy coming that was foretold or are we yet waiting for some other?' he replied by pointing to the features of his ministry which were foretold in two 'Messianic' texts of the Old Testament: 'Go and tell John what your own ears and eyes have witnessed; how the blind see, and the lame walk, and the lepers are made clean, and the deaf hear, how the dead are raised to life, and the poor have the gospel preached to them' (Mt. 11: 4 f., cf. Is. 35: 5, 61: 1).

In other words, though the claim of Jesus transcended anything that the Old Testament had led most Jews to expect, in making it he did so within the framework of Jewish ideas about the Chosen People. He wished to be accepted as the fulfilment of that People's Messianic hope. It may seem that he made little use, in reference to himself, of the title Messiah, and it may be that this term was dangerously mixed up with ideas of a 'kingdom of this world', so that he preferred not to make much of it. But the term Son of Man is very frequently on his lips, and this title too, like that of Messiah, was interwoven with the religious hopes of Israel as a people (cf. Dan. 7). Later strata of the New Testament are doubtless true to the spirit of his teaching when they describe him as 'saviour of the world' or 'saviour of all men'. But the means which he sought to adopt for the saving of all men was the conversion of the Chosen People. It is only when we fully realize this that we understand the depth of his sorrow when he was rejected by the officialdom of the Jews. The Messiah is inconceivable without the People of God, of which he is the *raison d'être*; the Son of Man is, in idea, an epitome of the 'people of the saints of God'. Yet the Chosen People, so far as the priests and Pharisees and scribes could be said to represent them, 'received him not' (Jn. 1: 11). The logic of the resultant situation is expressed in his prophecies of the overthrow of Judaism and its rejection by God, typified in the fall of Jerusalem and the destruction of the Temple. A Judaism which had rejected its Messiah had no more excuse for existing; it was an empty husk from which the life had departed, and the providence of God would no longer watch over it to save it from disaster.

Against this background of 'failure' and impending

c

retribution the acceptance of his claims by those who are referred to as his 'disciples' takes on its full significance. No doubt there were degrees of discipleship. Not all who had admired his teaching and wondered at his miracles were prepared to 'take up their cross and follow him' to the last extremes of martyrdom; and in fact at the moment of crisis even his specially chosen ones 'forsook him and fled'. But at least a minority, despite such momentary lapses, were devoted to him and his teaching, and would echo the words attributed to Simon Peter in the Fourth Gospel: 'Lord, to whom shall we go? Thy words are the words of eternal life' (6: 69). In the general scheme of the drama of his mission (which, of course, for the Christian believer, was not a failure but an inconceivably wonderful 'success'), these loyal followers were not just a few faithful individuals; they 'represented' Israel in a deeper sense than did the unbelieving officials—they were the nucleus of what St. Paul, appealing to the teaching of Old Testament prophecy, would one day call the 'remnant' of Israel. If Jesus was the Messiah, charged with the final and culminating revelation of God to his People, then from now onwards true membership of that People, considered not as a secular nation but as the covenanted collectivity, must depend on acceptance of his claim.

But a number of individual believers is not automatically a community. If the new Israel was to be the community of the Messiah, of the Son of Man, it must have some structure as a community. And in fact the Gospels show us Jesus selecting and gathering about himself a band of special followers to whom the title 'the Twelve' is early applied. That this group existed as a group before the crucifixion is guaranteed, as has been well observed, by the description of the traitor as 'one of the Twelve', and the reason for the number 'twelve' is suggested by the saying: 'You shall sit on twelve thrones . . . and shall be judges over the twelve tribes of Israel' (Mt. 19: 28)—in other words, here is the new authority, to take the place of the old officialdom, in the Chosen People. The leader of the Twelve, Simon son of Jonas, was given the significant title 'Rock' by Our Lord himself, so we are told by each of the four evangelists, and the saying in which he promises to 'build his Church on this rock' (Mt. 16: 18) is probably in substance authentic.[1] So also is the saying at the last supper with the Twelve: 'This is my blood of the covenant' (Mk. 14: 24); the Messiah establishes a new covenant with Israel, represented by its faithful remnant, in the person of these Twelve. Thus we see the New Israel taking shape in the womb of the old; a new

[1] Some doubt has been cast on Matthew 16: 18 in a recent article in the *Revue Biblique* by P. Denis, O.P. (October 1957). I have commented on his argument in 'St. Peter: History and Theology', *Clergy Review*, August 1958. It should be observed that 'Church' (ecclesia) is a word with an Old Testament background, suggesting the idea of God's people gathered in his presence.

fellowship, though *de jure* continuous with the old, centred in an embryonic 'hierarchy' and possessing, as it is presented to us in the Acts and the Epistles, the two great cultic rites of baptism and the Eucharist. When at length the predicted destruction of the Holy City and the Temple shattered the fabric of the historical Israel, the New Israel was already equipped as a society to take its place in world history as 'a light to enlighten the Gentiles'.

If, then, Christianity originates in a new revelation given by Jesus Christ, and if he refounded God's people Israel as the Church or the New Israel, we shall expect to find the element of Christian tradition to complete the trio: revelation, social recipient and tradition. Only once is it recorded of Jesus that he wrote; and it was in the dust of the earth (Jn. 8: 6). His teaching was by word of mouth; or rather it was the teaching of the friendly intercourse of master with disciples, extending beyond the spoken word to the total impression of personality on personalities—heart speaking to heart, to quote Newman's motto. The message or 'word' which the Twelve passed on to their converts after the Ascension was in fact a 'life': 'What we have heard . . . what our own eyes have seen of him, what it was that met our gaze and the touch of our hands' (1 Jn. 1: 1). A life, but also, as St. Paul says, a death: 'We preach Christ cruci-fied' (1 Cor. 1: 23). And this death was preached as a prelude to a resurrection from the dead: Matthias was chosen to take Judas's place and to be 'a witness of the resurrection' of Jesus (Acts 1: 22). Variations between the Gospels and other difficulties sometimes make us feel that it is impossible to get back to the actual words used by Jesus in his teaching. Perhaps it is a blessing in disguise that it is not easy to do so. It is true that as well as 'doing' and 'suffering' he taught. But it would seem that he taught not so much a new code of morality as a new spirit and a renewed ideal; and the actual words of a revered teacher so easily become a fetish. The seventh of the letters attributed to Plato has a passage about his philosophy which it does not seem irreverent to apply, *mutatis mutandis*, to the gospel of Jesus:

> No writing of mine on the subject exists, and there never will be one. It cannot be expressed in words like other subjects of instruction, but, as a result of frequent intercourse on the subject and of consorting together, it comes to birth in the soul like light enkindled from a leaping fire, and thereafter provides its own nourishment (341, c, d.).[1]

[1] For a Christian parallel we may compare the transmission of the spirit of St. Teresa of Avila to the Carmelites of the Reform: 'The perfection with which our holy mother (Teresa) founded her convents, wrote Quintanadoine to Mother Casilda, prioress of Valladolid, cannot be written in a set of constitutions or a book. Much rather, it consists in what she engraved in the hearts of those who saw her at work and had dealings with her; it was as it were something infused by God in their souls, to perpetuate this excellent and elevated mode of behaviour. Its main substance was an intimate and perfect communion with God and a great abstraction from creatures—and that, as I say, is something that cannot be written into the constitutions. In fact our constitutions

The same point may be illustrated by a passage from the eighteenth-century Jesuit de Caussade: 'The apostles' actions are governed less by the imitation of the deeds of Jesus than by the impression of his mind. Jesus Christ did not set limits to himself; he by no means followed all his maxims to the letter.' (*L'Abandon à la Providence Divine*, p. 92.) A contemporary non-Catholic scholar goes so far as to say: 'We cannot without extreme caution speak of any claim that Jesus made to be the Messiah: what claim he made was not explicit but implicit in his words and works.'[1]

It is to be expected *a priori* that a revelation not given in written, or indeed in merely verbal, form because it was a revelation in a life will have been transmitted in a 'tradition' which is more than written or verbal. And when we turn from Our Lord himself to the primitive Church we find again that the original appeal was not, so far as we can see, to written documents.[2] Few modern

are quite short. It is a spirit rather than a set of ceremonies.' Bremond, *Histoire Littéraire du Sentiment Religieux en France*, II, p. 309. As the spirit of St. Teresa lives on in the Reformed Carmelite convents, so the spirit of the gospel lives on in the Church.

[1] W. D. Davies, Mt. 5: 17–18, in *Mélanges Bibliques rédigés en l'Honneur d'André Robert*, p. 440. For an example of this implicit claim reference may again be made to Our Lord's reply to the two messengers of St. John the Baptist, Mt. 11: 5 f., where the virtual quotations from Isaiah 'imply' the claim to be Messiah. It is to be observed that an implicit claim can in fact be more impressive than an explicit one.

[2] In his *La Didachè, Instructions des Apôtres* (1958), J.-P. Audet claims to distinguish two strata in the *Didachè* (which he dates to about

scholars would admit (though the point is still arguable) that any of our extant New Testament books is earlier than 1 Thessalonians (*c.* A.D. 52) or possibly Galatians (at most about four years earlier): and by A.D. 52 the Church's leaders had been preaching the gospel for about twenty years. There may have been Christian literary activity before any of the New Testament books as we now have them was written; but there can be no doubt that the official teaching of the Church was primitively an oral teaching and proclamation, backed by the personal presence of the preacher, who, if he was one of the Twelve or of the wider group of 'apostles', was a living accredited eye-witness of the risen Jesus. And when at length the documents, now accepted as inspired New Testament literature, began to make their appearance it is possible in more than one of them to detect their dependence on the oral tradition. For instance, when we read (2 Thess. 2: 15) of 'the traditions you have learned, in word or writing, from us' we naturally think not only of 1 Thessalonians but of the oral instruction given to catechumens and neophytes. And when St. Paul refers to what he had himself 'received' and then 'handed on' to his Corinthian converts (1 Cor. 11: 23, 15: 1) it is again probable that oral transmission is in question. St. Mark's Gospel reads in

A.D. 50–70): an earlier one in which appeal is made to an oral tradition of Our Lord's teaching, and a later one of which the language implies that a written 'Gospel' is now available.

part like a record of the oral teaching of someone who
had been an eye-witness of Jesus's public life—probably
St. Peter. St. Luke undoubtedly had written sources
cf. 1: 1 ff.), but he probably supplemented them with
information derived orally and ultimately from eye-
witnesses. St. John's Gospel may have been in large
measure taught orally for many years before it was
committed to writing. In a brilliant study (*The Apostolic
Preaching*) C. H. Dodd has tried to reconstruct, so far as
possible, the contents of the oral proclamation of the
gospel in the earliest Church. More recently Riesenfeld
has argued that the tradition of the teaching of Jesus was
handed down by accredited and carefully taught oral
exponents. In fact it may be said that one of the major
preoccupations of present-day New Testament scholarship is to investigate and determine the oral tradition
lying behind the written New Testament.

We are indeed fortunate to possess, in the New
Testament documents, a fairly extensive collection of
written records of primitive Christianity; and the quality
of these records, considered simply as literature, is some
index of the immense spiritual dynamism of the move-
ment that sprang from the life, death, and resurrection
of Jesus. But at least for the independent historian it
must be an obvious presumption that the original tradition was far richer and more extensive than these records
are. And indeed it is impossible to understand the documents with any fullness unless we sketch in behind them,

admittedly with some element of conjecture, a background of unrecorded preaching, teaching, and living. We are inclined to think of a book as the creation of an individual author. We have to think of the New Testament books as products of a new form of communal believing, worshipping, and living. And we have to reconcile ourselves to the fact that what we know of Jesus Christ by historical research is what we can learn, with the help of the New Testament books, from the largely unwritten tradition of the Church of the apostolic age.

The independent historian will judge that not a little of the evidence of Christian origins and the primitive tradition in the New Testament has been almost accidentally preserved. St. Paul's account of the institution of the Eucharist in 1 Cor., which the prevailing opinion regards as earlier than any of the four Gospels, was occasioned, it would seem, not by a direct idea to give a piece of dogmatic teaching but by the wish to check what he regarded as practical abuses. And how much of the primitive tradition has been omitted? 'There is much else that Jesus did; if all of it were put in writing, I do not think the world itself would contain the books which would have to be written' (Jn. 21: 25). Modern scholars find it difficult to be sure that we have even a trustworthy framework of biography within which to serialize the incidents of Our Lord's ministry, and by the help of which to trace the development of his teaching and the unfolding of his missionary strategy. The earliest Christians had a profound interest in the history of their origins. How could they fail to have? Their whole message to the world, the whole reason of their existence as a religious collectivity, was bound up with the affirmation that Jesus had lived a historical life, had 'gone about' preaching and doing good, had risen from the dead, and had entrusted the apostles with the carrying forward of his work. But this interest was not precisely that which a modern critical historian has; it was not scientific but religious. This bald statement may require some qualification as regards St. Luke, for instance, who understood the idea of historical writing, not indeed as it is understood by a modern critic, but as the historians of the Graeco-Roman civilization understood it. He wrote, however, at a time when, as his Gospel shows, it was no longer possible to determine the course of events and their inner motivation with complete accuracy and fullness. To the other New Testament writers we may apply some words written recently about St. John in particular: 'He was not impelled to write by the inquisitiveness which prompts the modern historian . . . (St. John's) goal is the faith of his readers and the life which they will obtain through faith' (Grossouw, *Revelation and Redemption*, 1958). They wrote, in other words, 'from faith to faith', and what we find in their writings is not immediately the 'historical Jesus' but their convictions about him. Our modern New Testament study may be said to have started out on the *Quest of the Historical Jesus* (the English title of Albert Schweitzer's famous book); what it has in fact led to is the discovery of the primitive Church.

Meanwhile, we must not forget that the early transmission of the tradition of Christian origins was not confined to the New Testament writings. The non-written tradition, living in the life of the various local communities which made up the Church, was on the whole chronologically prior to the written books, and for a time it will have gone on playing its legitimate part alongside the written records, though gradually more and more influenced by them.[1] Papias, writing perhaps about A.D. 130–140, told how as a young man he had eagerly gleaned such information as he could from the followers of those who had seen Jesus. He even added, whether or not with reference to books of the New Testament: 'I thought that the contents of books were less serviceable to me than what could be derived from a living and continuing voice' (quoted, Eusebius, *H.E.*, iii. 39). More permanent than pure oral tradition were the usages and sacramental rites of the Church. These were not originally derived from the New Testament documents but preceded them. And rites and

[1] Cf. Audet's analysis of strata in the *Didachè*, p. 18, n. 1, *supra*. Whether this analysis is correct or not, it is most probable that this is the sort of way in which the written tradition came to take its place beside the unwritten.

usages have a very tough survival value. Perhaps hardly less important, though obviously incalculable, was the impression left on his original disciples, and passed on by them in the thousand and one indefinable means of communication available in the common life of a society, of the Founder of the Christian faith, the re-founder of the People of God. Irenaeus (*c.* A.D. 190) writes: 'Had the apostles left us no written information, would it not be necessary to follow the tradition of those to whom they entrusted the churches? This is the course followed by many races of barbarian believers, who without the help of ink and paper have salvation written in their hearts by faith and carefully preserve the ancient tradition' (*Adversus Haereses*, III, 4, 2).

A further observation is perhaps not irrelevant. Just as every trade or profession develops its own technical language and jargon, so too does a new, or a renewed, religion. So too of course do political traditions. New-man has a magnificent satirical passage portraying the outraged indignation of an imaginary foreigner who visits England and finds that it is a dogma of English law that 'the king can do no wrong' (*The Present Position of Catholics in England*, Lecture I). There is an apparently plain statement in six monosyllables which is very far from meaning what it appears to say; you have to read it in the context of a whole tradition in order to under-stand what it really means. Similarly in order to under-stand the New Testament books we have to try, by some means or other, to enter into the mind of the Church that produced them. Hoskyns and Davey, *The Riddle of the New Testament*, laid great stress on the way in which the new Christian experience and enlightenment twisted language from its normal orientation to express the new ideas and truths within a new systematic body of language.

In short we can say that the composition of the books which we now know as the New Testament did not put an end to the bond that links together revelation, religious community or society, and tradition. Written by adherents of the new faith and society, written from the angle of vision which was common to the members of that society, they were written for readers who were likewise its members, or for non-Christians who might be helped by them to attain to the same faith and to seek incorporation into the same society.

Can we now sum up the view that we can suppose an unbelieving historian would take of the place of the Bible in the Christian religion? The centre of the Christian faith, he would say, is the belief that Jesus of Nazareth was, in his person and his earthly history, the supreme and final revelation of God to man, summing up and raising to a higher level the alleged revelations of God to the people of Israel in pre-Christian times. The Old Testament books enable us in some degree to reconstruct for ourselves the developing religious education of the Israelite people, a process which they believed to have at its heart God's various utterances and self-disclosures through Moses and the prophets. By the beginning of the Christian era this process had reached a point at which the people as a whole, whether resident in Palestine or settled in the cities of the Roman Empire and the Near East, held the doctrine that Jahveh, their God, was the only God, the creator of the world and the source of the moral law; and the more advanced wing, represented for instance by the Pharisees in Palestine, also looked forward to the resurrection of the righteous dead, combining this belief in various ways with the general Jewish expectation of a future glorious establishment of the Reign of God through his people over the whole realm of history. Jesus's own teaching presupposed the truth of this general Jewish faith, including the article of the resurrection of the just dead. He addressed this teaching and his appeal to the Jewish people, and he claimed by implication to be the expected Messiah or Anointed One (Christ) who was to introduce the Reign of God. Rejected by official Judaism, he concentrated his attention upon those who accepted his claim, and gave to them the embryo of a constitution as the redeemed People of God or Messianic community, the New Israel which was to take the place of what St. Paul called 'Israel after the flesh', that is of the old Israel which, as represented at least by its official leaders, had rejected him. After his alleged resurrection this little society, with the Twelve at its head, continued to press his claim by the methods of oral teaching and preaching which he had himself employed and by direct personal appeal, summoning others to join their body as the community of the redeemed. They conducted their propaganda not only among the Jews but also among the pagan populations of the Roman Empire and contiguous territories. They were civilized people, though most of the earliest adherents were not highly educated, and they operated in a civilized milieu, and it was not long before a Christian literature—is literature not too grand a word?—began to be composed. These works were not originally written for ordinary sale in the bookshops of the Empire, but rather for private circulation within the Christian society. Much of what was written in the earliest days may well have disappeared irretrievably. But we have, in the so-called New Testament, a collection of Christian books which was given official status by the Church in a 'canon' or list which was itself substantially complete before the end of the second century. Of these official books the earliest are perhaps some of the epistles of St. Paul; and one at least of these was written within the first quarter of a century after the crucifixion of Christ. The latest of the Gospels was composed probably about A.D. 100; the earliest, it is usually held, was that of Mark, written perhaps about A.D. 67. The New Testament documents are an invaluable source for a reconstruction of the life and beliefs of the primitive Christian Church, and by a careful process of criticism we may hope to extract from them some idea of Jesus himself and his teaching. But what they purport to tell us about him is in the first instance evidence for their own beliefs—we make contact with Jesus Christ through the Church which he founded. The controlling factor, the link between Jesus and the New Testament books, is thus the Christian society, known from the earliest times as the *ecclesia* or Church—a name to which the title 'Catholic' or 'universal' began to be attached in the second Christian century.

I do not wish to suggest that believing Christians can rest content with the provisional, precarious, and changing verdicts of independent critics and historians, when it is a question of determining the foundations and the content of the faith. Far from it. A stream does not rise higher than its source, and if we were reduced to reliance on the fallible science of history, our faith could not have the firmness and certitude that we know it is meant to have. Just because we know this, the science of history points the believer beyond itself to a more trustworthy foundation. The question between traditional Protestantism and Catholicism is whether this foundation is 'the Bible and the Bible only', or whether it is the Church, out of whose life, so history tells us, the Bible sprang, and from whose judgment it derives its authority for us.

CHAPTER TWO

# Inspiration and Criticism

WE HAVE seen that the central conviction of Christianity is that Jesus the son of Mary was in his historical life the word of God to man. Other individuals in history, such as the prophets of ancient Israel, claimed to speak words of God; but for him it is claimed that he was the word of God. God's supreme revelation of himself and his will was not made in a series of statements like the articles of a Creed, nor in a code of moral precepts and prohibitions like the Ten Commandments. It was made in personal self-revelation, like the personal self-disclosure of a lover to his beloved. Love does not speak in terms of legal prescriptions or of philosophical theories. It outstrips language and is manifested in facial expression, in gesture, in silence and in listening, in action and also in suffering. If we want to know how Christianity conceives God's revelation of himself to us, we may turn to those wonderful chapters of St. John's Gospel which purport to describe Jesus's last hours with his faithful few before his arrest and crucifixion. We do not find there such technicalities as are contained in the famous formula of the General Council of Chalcedon (A.D. 451), which defined that Our Lord had the complete nature of God and a complete human nature, joined without confusion in the unity of a single divine person. Such definitions, when ratified by the supreme authority of the Church, are of course true to the implications of the revelation; but it was not originally given in such formulas. What we read in St. John is how Jesus girded himself with a towel and washed the feet of his disciples; how he poured out his heart to them in the urgency of the knowledge that his time was now very short—there was so much to say, and even if there had been time to say it, it was beyond their present grasp (16: 12); how he realized their dismay and depression and gently rallied them to confidence and hope; how he allowed them to express, in their turn, what he himself had taught them: their overriding desire to be shown God; and how he met this desire with the tremendous affirmation: 'Whoever has seen me, has seen the Father' (14: 9). 'I do not speak of you any more as my servants. . . . I have called you my friends' (15: 15). That is the heart of the Christian revelation; provided we remember that the word 'friend' is used here in the fullest, deepest sense that we can possibly put upon it—not the friendship of business partners or boon companions or even of comrades in arms, but a friendship of which the core is the profoundest love coupled with the profoundest respect and esteem.

Now let us take up the attitude, not of independent historians of religion, but of men and women who believe in the Christian faith. The question then for us is as follows. Since Jesus Christ in his historical life on earth is God's supreme and final word to man, to all men and to each man, to each of us here and now, how does that word speak itself to us individually? It is part of our Christian conviction that to hear and respond to the word of God is our single all-embracing task here below; that without it our life is but an idiot's tale. What more terrible threat could we hear than that which we read in Amos 8: 11 f.?

A time is coming, says the Lord God, when there shall be great lack in the land, yet neither dearth nor drought. Hunger? Ay, they shall hunger for some message from the Lord, yet go they from eastern to western sea, go they from north to south, making search for it everywhere, message from the Lord they shall have none.

Our question is not a bit of mere theory, an amusement for an idle mind. The whole of our destiny hangs on the answer to it.

And of course the fundamental answer to it is beyond doubt. Having chosen a human means of revealing himself—nothing less than a human nature and a historical human life—God has chosen that our knowledge of his revelation, since we do not live in Palestine in the first half-century of our era, should be mediated to us

by human means; by means of what, in the previous
chapter, we have called 'tradition'. You will remember
that I used this word to cover both unwritten memories,
monuments and memorials, and the written word. In
this sense of the word we reminded ourselves that
tradition is part and parcel of the continuing, developing, and continuously identical, life and culture of
human society. History may be called the story of man
in society, and God has chosen to give us a historical
revelation in Jesus Christ; so tradition mediates, transmits, that revelation to us.

Where do we find this tradition? Almost exclusively in
Christian sources. There is practically nothing in either
Jewish or pagan tradition that adds anything of moment
to what the Christian sources have to tell us of Christ—
of Christ himself, as distinct from the historical context
in which his life on earth was lived. Usually, I think,
whatever is reliable in these non-Christian sources may
be itself derived from Christian information, though it
is possible that the Jewish historian Josephus (c. A.D. 90)
may have had knowledge of the existence of Jesus from
Jewish sources, and it is just possible that Tacitus, the
Roman historian, who mentions Pontius Pilate's execution of Christ to explain who were the 'Christians' who
were blamed for the fire of Rome under Nero, got this
fact from the Acta of the Senate, or from an earlier
Roman writer Pliny the Elder, who had been in Palestine during the Jewish rebellion of A.D. 66–70. But we

have to remember that the execution of an alleged political agitator of no military significance in an unimportant province was not a fact to cause more than at most a ripple of interest in the capital of the Empire. The Church itself, for Tacitus in the early years of the second century, was just another of those disgusting Eastern superstitions which naturally found their way sooner or later to Rome, the centre and microcosm of a culture that was anything but homogeneous. Christianity's Jewish antecedents were not calculated to recommend it to an admirer of Rome's aristocratic traditions.

So we ask, what are the Christian sources in which we make our contact with Christ, with God revealed in Christ, with God's supreme word to us men? The Protestant answer appears to be that they are simply and solely the books of the New Testament. And I think that most old-fashioned Protestants would have regarded these books as inspired. In fact, it is probably true to say that the inspiration of Scripture is part of the Protestant tradition, although a recent writer speaks no doubt for a large body of modern Protestant thought (at least in scholarly circles) when he implies that we can hardly be confident that the Old Testament writings are the inspired word of God.[1] The Reformers protested against and rejected a great deal in the Catholicism of their age. But of course they took over from it a

[1] E. W. Heaton, *The Old Testament Prophets*, 1958, p. 14.

great deal too. And one of the things they retained, and shared with Catholicism, was belief in the authority of Scripture; and with it the Canon or list of the New Testament books and that of what are called the proto-canonical books of the Old Testament (that is to say the books which the Jews also regard as canonical literature). It is a historical fact that both the canon of Scripture and the doctrine that Scripture's authority is incontest-able (which we explain by the doctrine of inspiration) are Catholic things. Just as we owe the existence and the handing down of the New Testament books to the primitive Church, whose faith they enshrine and of which their authors were members, so also it is to the Church of the second and later centuries that we owe our list of canonical New Testament books, our accep-tance of the Old Testament books as canonical, and our faith that all these books are inspired by the Holy Ghost and are therefore authoritative in the matter of religion. I think it has always been something of an embarrass-ment to Protestantism, which rejects the doctrinal authority of the Church, to justify its acceptance of the canon of Scripture and of the belief that Scripture is of final authority, or even inspired.[1] The Westminster

[1] I do not know whether the word 'inspired' is found in any Protes-tant confessions of belief. It is curiously absent from the Anglican XXXIX Articles. I think it is indisputable that the old-fashioned Protestant attitude to Scripture as the word of God implies a belief in inspiration.

Confession (1647) maintained that we are convinced of the truth of what we read in Scripture by the inward work of the Holy Spirit bearing witness by and with the word in our hearts.[1] I hope it is not merely flippant to say that few of us can be confident that this inward witness by itself would suffice to assure us of the inspiration of the Books of Chronicles or of the Epistle of St. James, which latter, I understand, caused some difficulty to Luther; or that while assuring us of the inspiration of the Song of Songs it fails to convince us of that of the Book of Wisdom—which latter, as being only deutero-canonical, is not regarded by Protestantism as authoritative for doctrine (cf. the XXXIX Articles on the 'Apocrypha', i.e. the deutero-canonical books). Nor of course can the Bible itself satisfy us either of its own pervasive inspiration, or of the exact contents of its own canon. The tendency of modern Protestant liberalism is to give up the doctrine of inspiration, as may be seen from the opinion of Canon Heaton mentioned above and possibly also from the *Basis and Plan of Union* (1929): 'The Church of Scotland acknowledges the Word of God which is contained in the Scriptures'—this phrase seems to suggest that Scripture is not itself the word of God, but that diligent search can extract that word from Scripture. This tendency may be true to the interior logic of a religion of private judgment.

[1] I owe this information to 'Our Separated Brethren in Scotland', an unpublished paper by R. Walls.

But when it goes hand in hand with a rejection of the doctrinal authority of the Church it is likely to lead either to intellectual antinomianism or to the tyranny of scholarship. I hope to say something later on about the grave motives that have led so many scholars to this kind of liberalism. For the moment, and for the sake of argument, I want to assume that it is agreed that in some sense the Bible is the inspired word of God.

The Catholic Church, for its part, points to not one but two sources of our knowledge of the contents of the Christian revelation, our knowledge of the Word Incarnate: the Bible, but also what, in distinction from this written source, the Council of Trent calls 'unwritten traditions'. The latter phrase need not mean simply an oral transmission of things which could equally well have been set down in the books of the Bible; it may cover also such things as the sacramental rites of the Church, and in general the transmissible contents of what is sometimes called 'the mind of the Church'. As I have previously argued, tradition is something wider than language.

Catholic acceptance of these two sources of knowledge of the faith brings us up against a question which is still under dispute among Catholic theologians. Let me explain. As we saw in the first chapter, the Church's tradition existed before most of the New Testament books were written—presumably before any of them were. The books themselves were written at various dates down to A.D. 100 or later. While they were in process of being written the unwritten tradition of course went on. It was what the Twelve had been commissioned to hand on to their converts, and what we may presume their successors in the government of the Church continued, after the apostles' death, to hand on. There were thus two sources of tradition, existing side by side: the written books which we now call the New Testament, and the continuing unwritten tradition in the practice of the Church and the teaching of its commissioned ministers; this second source, of course, was subject to the influence of the written books in so far as they were known and their authority acknow-ledged. As we have seen, Irenaeus, near the end of the second century, though he vehemently rejected the alleged secret traditions of the Gnostics, yet suggested that even without the written books we could still know the saving truth by appeal to the tradition of the Church. The Catholic Church, then, still today points to these two streams of tradition.

It is obvious that the two sources of tradition can overlap. Thus the Church teaches that Jesus Christ is the Son of God. She knew this before the earliest books of the New Testament were written, if we accept the ordinary scholarly dating of these books. She would have remembered and taught it, we may hold, even if the books had never been written. But the books do also themselves teach us this truth. Now the question is: Is there anything in the contents of the 'unwritten' tradition over and above what can be discovered in the Bible itself? The conservative Protestant view is that the Bible contains all things necessary for salvation; that is to say that the whole Christian revelation has been embodied in the Bible. It is often thought, and Catholics themselves have often given the impression, that the Catholic Church denies this to be the case, and maintains on the contrary that there are things which belong to the original revelation and are 'of faith' which cannot in any sense be found in the Bible. It must be stated emphatically that the Church has made no definite pronouncement to this effect. The Council of Trent did not define that revelation is contained partly in the Bible and partly in unwritten tradition; it only defined that both these are sources from which revelation (whether all or only some revelation) can be recovered. And there is a fairly widely held view among modern Catholic theologians that in fact there is nothing in the unwritten tradition that is not also in some sense discoverable in the Bible. This view was presented as a possibility by Newman in his answer to Pusey's *Eirenicon* (*Difficulties of Anglicans*, vol. II).[1] It is important to remember that it is in no sense unorthodox.

[1] Cf. the following from J. B. Kuhn, a pupil of Möhler, in 1858: 'In the entire early age of the Church we can find no dogmatic formulation for which there is not at least some premise or starting-point in Scripture.' Scripture, says J. R. Geishmann (*Lebendige Glaube aus*

The contrary view, on the other hand, has some arguments in its favour. To begin with, it is impossible to draw up a canon of Scripture from the internal evidence of the Bible itself without appeal to any outside evidence or authority. How should we know, for instance, by merely examining the books of the Bible, whether the Second Epistle of St. Peter is to be reckoned in the Bible or not? Of course Catholics know the answer, because the Church tells them that it is canonical and therefore inspired. But how does the Church know this? She is guided to her decision by the Holy Ghost: 'It will be for him, the truth-giving Spirit, when he comes, to guide you into all truth' (Jn. 16: 13). But this decision, though guided by God, is based on evidence which is, or has at some time in the past been, available. The evidence is not in the pages of the Bible itself, so far as we can see, at least, not sufficient evidence. It therefore seems that we must call in the evidence of the 'unwritten' tradition in order that the scope and limits of the canon of Scripture may be decided by the Church.[1] Secondly, the books of the New Testament do not convey the impression of having been intended to gather together into a single complete whole all that the

*geheiligter Uberlieferung,* cf. *Una Sancta II,* 1956) is dogmatically complete—it gives the starting-point or indications which tradition explains and applies.

[1] For those non-Catholics who accept the authority of the Bible but reject that of the Church, the problem is obviously not capable of solution along these lines.

apostles had learnt from the Word Incarnate and from
his revealing Spirit during their lifetime. They look like
a haphazard collection of books, all indeed written under
the stimulus of the new revelation, but written at different times, by various writers, and for very varying
purposes. Some of their most richly doctrinal passages
appear to have been written not for the purpose of
teaching doctrine but for that of moral exhortation
based on doctrine already familiar to their readers. If it
is to be maintained that, above and beyond the purposes
of the individual writers, there was a divine purpose to
include in these books everything that was part of the
revelation in Jesus Christ, must it not be admitted that
this purpose cannot be deduced from a study of the
books themselves? And for the discovery of this purpose
should we not therefore have to turn either to the unwritten tradition, or to theological inferences which are
not necessarily cogent, or, more immediately, to the
Church's authority? As regards the latter, it is quite true
that the Church has given a highly privileged place to
Scripture by teaching that it is inspired by the Holy
Ghost. And it is very interesting to see how, when a
doctrine is defined by the Church, she regularly seeks
to find a basis for it in Scripture. But as she still, at
present, leaves us free to hold that there are elements of
the deposit of faith which have been preserved in their
fullness only by the single channel of unwritten tradition, some no doubt will continue to find the opinion

more consonant with *a priori* probabilities. The fundamental revelation in Jesus Christ, the Word of God made flesh, was given, as has already been remarked, in a personal contact with the disciples (the embryo Church) that overflowed language—in smile and gesture and deed as well as in the spoken word; and the revelation so given was transmitted primitively in similar fashion. It may seem to some people improbable that this lived revelation could have been totally recorded in the written word; it would be like supposing that a poet could fully express himself in his poetry. In any case it is certain that the written word itself can only be fully understood within the continuance of the unwritten tradition. All Catholic theologians would presumably agree with Newman that not every article of faith is so contained in Scripture that it may thence be logically proved, independently of the teaching and authority of the unwritten tradition (*Difficulties of Anglicans*, II, p. 12).

It is time to turn from this unsolved problem about tradition to the conviction, common, I hope, to us and to the more conservative of our Protestant friends, that the Bible is inspired by the Holy Ghost. The Vatican Council explains this as meaning that the books of the Bible 'have God as their author'. There is plainly something that needs consideration here, since it is obvious that each of these books has also a human author or authors. How can the same book have both God and man as its author? It is not as though the Holy Ghost had simply 'dictated' the words of the book to a human being who acted simply as a sort of amanuensis. A novelist might have three different shorthand typists working for him at different times, but his style would be much the same whichever typist he was employing. But the styles of the New Testament books vary widely. St. Paul is an author whose fiery generous temperament and profound mind we get to know intimately as we read his epistles. He is quite different from the piercing-eyed contemplative St. John of the Johannine epistles and of the Gospel. And each of these is very different again from the cultured kindly tender St. Luke and the systematic prosaic St. Matthew. The human authors, then, are real authors, putting themselves into their books, not just secretaries writing to divine dictation.

It may be worth while to try to think out a theory of inspiration together. The Church does not teach that part of the contents of the Epistle to the Galatians comes from Paul, and part from the Holy Ghost. She says that it all comes from the Holy Ghost. And we say that it all comes from St. Paul. In other words, the same result, namely the book in its totality, comes from the human author, but also, on a higher level of reality, from the divine author, the Holy Ghost. The Holy Ghost does not just use the penmanship of the human author (who, anyhow, probably often used another human being as his secretary); he uses the human author as an author, to be the living, thinking, freely willing, instrument by which he, the Holy Ghost, utters his mind to us.

We might try an analogy—not a complete parallel, but a suggestive comparison—with what theology tells us about God as the cause of everything that happens. That is the basis of our belief in divine providence. We believe that any action of a creature, in the full measure of its reality as an act, is also, but in a higher sense, an effect of divine action; God is not only the one source of the being of things, he is the unmoved source of all motion, of all action. When I raise my arm I am of course acting and am causing my arm to rise. But in a higher sense God causes that effect as he also causes my existence. Every creaturely action is in a deeper sense, then, a result of God's action; and God's action is identical with himself. Yet we know that we have no feeling of being interfered with in our acting by God's action. I am fully my own master in acting (I could refuse to perform this particular action); yet without God's concurrent action I could not even begin to act. In a similar way I suggest that God's inspiration of an author is not necessarily something of which the human author is aware as an interference or an uplift; not necessarily something of which he is aware at all.

Now, however, we must remind ourselves that we have only been offering an analogy; we have not given an explanation. God is of course the ultimate cause of

all the books of the New Testament, just as he is the
ultimate cause of all other human productions—of the
plays of Shakespeare, for instance. But even though, in
a loose sort of way, we talk of Shakespeare as an inspired
poet, we do not mean that God is the author of the
plays of Shakespeare. Why not? Because a work of
literature, just like any other human writing or spoken
utterance, has a meaning. That is not the case with all
human acts; not all of them have meaning. When I put
out my arm when driving a car to signal that I am
about to turn right, the act has a meaning, because it is
intended as a sign. But when I raise my arm to brush a
fly from my face, the act has no meaning; it has a
purpose, but that is not quite the same thing. We use
language, then, both in speech and in writing books, to
express meaning. Language is a kind of signs. Now
when we so use language, God is no doubt the cause of
our action as a physical action, but he does not necessarily identify himself with the meaning of our utterance; he does not make our affirmation his or accept
responsibility for it. And it appears that what the Church
intends by her doctrine of the inspiration of Scripture is
that the meaning of the inspired authors is God's meaning too; that in this case he does take responsibility for
the meaning. Thus, if we can determine what St. John
meant when he wrote, in his first epistle, 'God is love',
then we shall know that that meaning is also God's. On
the other hand, we may know what Nelson meant by

his signal: 'England expects every man to do his duty'; but we do not know that Nelson's meaning was God's meaning, or that God meant anything by the signal, although God was the ultimate cause of it.[1]

From the doctrine of the inspiration of Scripture it is commonly inferred that Scripture is inerrant. In other words, what the authors of the several books of the Bible asserted in these books is true. God cannot be the author of false meaning. He cannot lie, and he is the divine author of these books.

As soon as we have said this we are brought up against the formidable difficulties that have led many non-Catholic scholars to give up the doctrine of inspiration, or at least to reduce it to something which is no longer recognizable as the traditional doctrine. These difficulties are specially, but by no means exclusively, connected with the Old Testament, and some of them have forced themselves on our attention as a result of the expert criticism to which the Bible has been subjected during the last hundred and fifty years. Three groups of difficulties may be distinguished: the morality of some passages, especially in the Old Testament, seems reprehensible to our modern conscience; Scripture seems to be full of statements which are untrue; and

---

[1] It will be observed that I have been offering not simply a statement of the doctrine of inspiration, but an interpretation of it. The doctrine is of course authoritative; there is nothing authoritative about my interpretation.

B

many of the books of the Bible seem to owe their final
form to editors rather than authors—which of the
human agents behind a given book is to be held to have
been the inspired writer? I will not spend much time
over this last difficulty, as it impresses the imagination
more than the reason. It is obviously possible, so far as
we can see, for inspiration to intervene at the last stage
of editing, so that the book as it at length goes to take
its place in the canon of Scripture may represent not
only the final labours of the member of the believing
community who 'prepared it for publication' but also
the real intention of God in whose eternal providence
it was destined for canonical status.

The second sort of difficulty is more considerable. To
take an obvious and well-known example: the Old Testament seems to offer a system of chronology from which
it may be deduced that the first man was created about
6,000 years ago; my copy of the Douai Version, in fact,
has a footnote on Gen. 1: 1 which appears to indicate
that the world was created in 4004 B.C. But archaeology
and anthropology have made it practically certain that
man has existed on earth for a vastly longer period than
this, and it is suggested by some scientists that the
material universe has been in existence for about 4,000
million years. Again, the attempts which have been
made to harmonize the account of creation in Genesis
with scientific theories of evolution and cosmogony
must be said to have failed. Criticism again finds reasons

for thinking that the Old Testament books have on occasion read back into earlier periods conditions that only became actual, if at all, in later ages. One could go on almost indefinitely. Conservative Christian scholars, whether Catholics or not, have often tried to resist the verdicts of criticism in order to preserve their own view of the inerrancy and inspiration of Scripture. Criticism of course has made and still makes its mistakes, like any other science—we all remember the Piltdown skull. But taking the broadest possible view, I think it must be said that in the long run no conservatism would suffice to meet validly the challenge of criticism along these lines. There comes a point beyond which conservatism earns the less honourable name of obscurantism: the refusal to face facts. So I want to put before you a different way of dealing with this set of difficulties.

I suggest that it may be helpful to remember that a statement in words, whether spoken or written, does not always assert precisely what in grammar it says. Let me give an example, which I hope you will not think too absurdly elementary. My morning paper states: Sun rises 4.55 a.m. Taken grammatically, that statement would seem to imply that the earth is stationary relative to the sun, and that the sun goes round the earth, a theory which has been out of favour with scientists for quite a long time. But I do not suppose that the editor of *The Times* really holds the theory which his use of language might seem to imply. And

notice that my paper always gives an exact minute—
neither a few seconds before nor a few seconds after—
for the sun to appear in the morning. An astronomer
might object that this was inaccurate and false; but then
I know that the editor is not pretending to astronomical
accuracy. His statement about the sun conforms to
accepted conventions of speech and of approximate
accuracy, and it has to be read in the light of those
conventions if we are to distinguish between what it
says 'in so many words' and what it is intended to assert.
This is a trivial example, but we can plainly apply it on
a big scale to the Bible, by making allowance for the
conventions within which the writers wrote and trying
thus to penetrate beyond the literal word to what they
were intending to tell us, that is to what God is intending to tell us. Here I think we have the crucial question
in dealing with our difficulty: what is the author intending to assert? It will not always be an easy question
to answer, but until we have answered it, how can we
say that the assertions of Scripture are contradicted by
science or critical history? None of the sacred books
presents itself as a scientific treatise, so we need not
suppose that God intends to offer us scientific information anywhere in the Bible.

Take the first chapter of Genesis again. The author is
saying a great deal. But what is he trying to assert? It
may reasonably be doubted whether he is trying to
assert anything more than that God is the creator of

heaven and earth and all things in them; that he is the
source of all goodness as of all being in things; that
there are degrees of worth in things, and that man stands
above all other worldly things as in a special sense
reflecting the nature of God. To express these truths the
author accepts the conventions of language, thought,
and belief of his day. He writes as though the earth was
shaped like a flat loaf, with the sky poised above it like
the lid of a tureen; and as though creation took place
in a period of six days of twenty-four hours each; and
all this he may have 'believed'. But he need not be taken
as asserting these beliefs, any more than the editor of a
daily paper, even if he had been writing before the days
of Copernicus, need have been asserting his belief in
the centrality of the earth when he used conventional
language to tell us the time of what we still call sunrise.
A speaker in Parliament may spend a quarter of an hour,
2,000 words, and a great deal of exaggerated rhetoric,
to make a single point that could have been expressed
in a sentence of twenty words.

So our first question, when we are seeking for the
bearing of inerrancy on Scripture, is: what is the human
author intending to tell us; because this will be what
God is intending to tell us.

And here it is important to remember that, like
modern natural science, scientific historical scholarship
and its literary conventions are modern developments.
They have some precedent in ancient Greek history-

writing from Thucydides onwards. But to put Thucydides on a level with Trevelyan or Napier would be not altogether unlike putting Aristotle on a level with Einstein in the sphere of physical science. Thucydides and his readers knew, in a general sort of way, something of the limitations of historical science in their own day; so we may imagine, if we like, that Thucydides was not committing himself to the literal detailed truth of all he wrote to quite the same extent as Trevelyan does today. Even Trevelyan would be treated rather hardly if we tried to make him personally responsible for the exact truth of every sentence in his books; does he not often repeat, as 'taken for granted', the traditional account? Have you ever tried to prove that the Battle of Hastings took place in A.D. 1066? And if someone came along and proved that it was actually in 1057, would you accuse all previous historians of lying, because they repeated without qualification the traditional date? If I say that there were something over 17 million people in England in 1851, is it supposed that I claim to have been there and to have counted them? No; everyone recognizes that I am probably giving the figure that I have found in an author whom I judge to be reasonably reliable.

The Old Testament 'historical writers' had not learnt their trade from Trevelyan; they had not even learnt it from Thucydides. We might say that they were more like Herodotus, or more like Homer; saga-poets, bards, patriotic poets, rather than scientific historians. If you take in hand to retell with a religious colouring the national and tribal legends that have whiled away the fireside winter hours which are fit neither for fighting nor for farming, it is not fair that you should be judged as a witness in a court of law. Was it not Samuel Johnson's dictum, that a writer of epitaphs is not to be conceived as one giving evidence under oath?

Of course, large parts of the Old Testament do not pretend to be historical records at all. The Psalms are not history but religious hymns—they are poetry (not that the distinction between prose and poetry was quite so marked in ancient Israel as it was in modern Britain before the days of free verse and post-Eliot poetry). What exactly does poetry assert? What was Shakespeare asserting when he wrote: Shall I compare thee to a summer's day? Thou art more lovely and more temperate. And if the Psalms are poetry, finding room for an occasional bit of mythology as poetry is so ready to do, the Book of Job is more like Aeschylus than Caesar's *Commentaries*. May we not add that the books of Tobias and Jonas are rather like *The Pilgrim's Progress*? We do not ask whether Bunyan's hero really existed; rather we know that, in a sense beyond that of scientific history, he is you and I.

Thus we have been led on to the subject of what are nowadays called 'literary types'.[1] If we are seeking to

[1] I use this phrase to translate *genera litteraria*, which means 'kinds of literature'; a convenient English translation is not easy to contrive.

determine the truth, if any, that the author of a book intended to convey, and to which he wished to commit his own credit, we have to consider and bear in mind the conventions of the class or type of literature to which the book belongs. And in the case of an ancient writer, the determination of these conventions may be a matter of no little scholarship and delicacy of insight. Here it may be well to remind ourselves again that the books which got included in the canon of Scripture were put there for their religious value, not for their value in respect of profane information or secular interests. As they were canonized for their religious value, so too they had usually been written, or finally edited, for a religious purpose. In a sense, then, we might say that all the books of the Bible belong to one supreme literary family, that of religious literature.

For an illustration of the use to which one may put the notion of literary types, let us turn for a moment from the Old to the New Testament. When St. Luke wrote the Acts of the Apostles he probably thought of himself, to some extent, as writing within the conventions of the Greek historical writers of the period. It has often been debated whether history is a science or an art. In ancient times, it may be claimed, it was more of an art than it is today. St. Luke will have thought of himself, I therefore suggest, rather as a portrait or landscape painter than as an official photographer. If you have artistic education and sensibility, you do not blame

El Greco for not getting the proportions of the anatomy of his painted figures correct; you know that he was not trying to do so. So if it seems, when criticism has done its best or worst, that St. Luke has, for instance, combined two different episodes in his story of the Council at Jerusalem, we need not cry in despair that the doctrine of inspiration has been proved to be false. Instead, we shall ask ourselves whether, within the limits of the convention that St. Luke has adopted for his book, the combination is legitimate or not. And again I would add that St. Luke had the literary traditions not only of Greece but of Israel behind him; he was writing sacred literature, and he was certainly not writing with the scientific apparatus and claims of a modern professional historian.

It may be asked, perhaps with some alarm: Are you going to apply this principle of literary types to the Gospels? Yes, I am. It is a principle universally applicable to human use of language for purposes of communication. Whether we speak or we write, we are communicating by means of language, which is a set of conventional signs. The same thing can mean different, even opposite, things according to the convention which is being followed. 'I could eat you' may mean an expression of affection or the contrary.

But if we go on to ask what convention the evangelists were following we are met by a fresh difficulty. Plainly, each of them intended to present Christ to his readers. But what was the appropriate convention for this task? The reply is not quite obvious. If you thought of Christ as primarily a teaching prophet, you might turn for models to the Old Testament books of the prophets. If you thought of him primarily as a miracle-worker, you might turn to the stories of Elias and Elisaeua in the Books of Kings. If as a martyr, to the story of the Maccabean martyrs. But Christ was not primarily any of these, or rather he was all these and more than all; he was something new. What the primitive Church implicitly thought about him is made explicit in the Johannine formulation: 'The Word was made flesh.' Sayings, miracles, passion, resurrection, even birth and childhood were all relevant: and yet a mere chronicle, putting every event of his life on the same level, would fail to bring out the truth. So the Gospels are, it may be claimed, a new type of literature; we cannot put them without more ado into any pre-existing category. Our task is to find out the pattern which they embody, and its sub-patterns, and thence the intention of the writers, from internal evidence.

In fact, of course, the resort to internal evidence is necessary for the understanding of any book in which the author has played a fully creative part. Precisely to the extent to which the author is an author, we have not fully characterized the pattern of his work or discovered his intention by assigning his work to a given literary type. A type is a general category. But a work of literature, like any other work of art, is concrete and individual. A real author is not the slave of the type he has, consciously or unconsciously, adopted. He makes it his servant. In the last resort we can only understand what he is trying to tell us by 'getting into' his individual mind. The New Testament writers share the common faith of the Church and wrote, as we have said, from it and to it; they are anything but modern critics. And being men of a particular age and subject to particular cultural influences, they were influenced by already existing conventions of literary expression. But each has also his own outlook, his own intention; each gives the individual form of his own mind to what he writes. We have to learn to sympathize with his outlook in order to penetrate to his intention.

What, then, as you may impatiently ask, is the truth 'behind' the books of the Bible, as modern critics understand the word 'truth'? That sort of desiccated 'scientific' truth was not the immediate concern of the Biblical writers. If we want it, we must turn from them to the modern critics themselves, or ourselves become modern critics. And of course criticism's answers to our questions are always provisional, precarious you might say. We must not demand from criticism a clearer and more detailed finality than it has it in its power to offer; if we do, it will break under the strain that is laid upon it and will become sceptical. We may hope that certain broad outlines of truth may appear through the mists of time, and we must be content, very often, with what is sometimes called 'moral certainty', even though we hanker after metaphysical certainty.

Meanwhile, we can take comfort by reminding ourselves that the basic faith of the New Testament writers and of the Church to which they belonged was that salvation had historically happened in a particular life lived in Palestine in the period from Herod the Great to Pontius Pilate. The Church could echo the words of the Nunc Dimittis: 'My own eyes have seen that saving power of thine which thou has prepared in the face of all nations' (Luke 2: 29 f.). Thus the primitive Church was quite sure that Our Lord had risen from the dead. St. Paul speaks not only for himself when he affirms that 'if Christ has not risen, all your faith is a delusion' (1 Cor. 15: 17). The Word had become incarnate and 'we had sight of his glory' (Jn. 1: 14); 'our eyes have seen' and 'our hands have touched' him (1 Jn. 1: 1). The primitive Church was not content to say that something had happened; it bore witness, it pointed to eye-witnesses of what had happened among its own commissioned leaders. Again, we can see from 1 Cor. 7: 10 ('For those who have married already, the precept holds which is the Lord's precept, not mine; the wife is not to leave her husband etc.') that what Christ had ordered had prescriptive force for the early Church. This would mean that if you started repeating, as though it were a normative word of Christ, something that he had never said there would be someone with knowledge and interest to protest. More broadly, the Twelve based their leadership of the Church on the commission they had received to propagate Christ's gospel. Even if they had wished to resort to their own invention, there were plenty of people about, inside and outside the Church, who had enough knowledge to serve as a general check upon them. It is precisely about the primitive Church, as I said earlier, that our New Testament studies are beginning to tell us something; and so far as we can see the primitive Church regarded this gospel as a sacred 'word' of God, and would have adopted an attitude towards it not less respectful than that of the rabbinic schools to their traditions. In other words, and speaking in general, the faith and thought which moulded the New Testament literature presupposed the truth of the material which that literature gave shape to; truth, I repeat, in the broad sense of that term, not in the narrow scientific sense of modern critical scholarship. The primitive Church was not a group of starry-eyed adherents of a mystery-cult with a myth unrelated to historical happening. It was a fellowship of passionately convinced, very realistic, much given to controversy, and (so far as we can judge) pretty honest men and women, who, in the earlier period, were mainly converts from Judaism. There is nothing like controversy to make you watch the accuracy of what you say!

All this, however, is a bit beside the point as far as

concerns the precise question of the inspiration of Scripture. I have said that the common inference from the doctrine of inspiration is that Scripture is inerrant; that what it tells us is true. And I have been trying to meet, without obscurantism, the objection that a great deal, especially but not exclusively, of the Old Testament is not true as modern critical historians understand the word 'true'. My reply is, that we have to discover what the Biblical authors were severally trying to tell us; in other words, what was their intention: what did they intend to assert? I argue that we should treat them as we treat the editor of a newspaper looking beyond, or through, the verbal forms they use to the point of their meaning; which we can hope to discover, up to a point, by a deeper understanding of the literary types to which they conform. We have to try to put our minds back into a world in which scientific historical criticism and the standards it imposes were virtually unknown, a world in which (again especially when we are dealing with the Old Testament) poetry and saga and legend, even on occasion myth, were legitimate vehicles of the transmission of one's meaning to others. I agree that all this may mean a very considerable re-thinking of the implications of the doctrine of inspiration. But that is not to suggest that we need surrender to the easy but disastrous expedient of jettisoning the doctrine itself. Theology is always renewing itself, when it is alive and healthy. But doctrine and dogma stand firm and are in themselves, though not in our understanding of them, unalterably true.

We have still a third difficulty to face. Our modern, Christianly educated, conscience is revolted by a good deal of what we read, especially in the Old Testament. And we find it particularly revolting when some frightful thing, like the massacre of the pre-Israelite inhabitants of Canaan, is said to have been commanded by God. Can God command what is evil?

How are we to reply to this objection? I think we can turn to the notion of development. The Old Testament is a record, by and large, of the gradual age-long education of the Chosen People in the nature and claims of the God of righteousness who had vouchsafed to be 'their' God. This educative process did not take place within the closed walls of a monastery but in the conditions of a national life lived out in the full glare of history. Nor were the souls of the Israelites a sort of blank page, with no religious or ethical conceptions, pre-conceptions, to be either obliterated or corrected, purified, elevated and enlarged. They were a group of Semitic clans, gradually taking shape as a united people, and unfortunately, after Solomon's death, as two united peoples: the northern and the southern kingdoms. These peoples were intensely self-centred, but were also exposed through long periods of their history to the influence of the splendid and seductive nature-religions of their Canaanite neighbours, and later to the religions of the great world-empires. Their own faith and religious practice, gradually elaborated from the days of Moses through the age of the great prophets and on into post-exilic times, were at once a protest against, and in some respects a transposition of, surrounding beliefs and practices. It would be asking too much to expect them to reflect at all times the exalted morality of the Sermon on the Mount.

Suppose we take the story of the proposed sacrifice of Isaac by his father Abraham in illustration of the point I am trying to make. The sacrifice of children to the local Baal was a feature at once tremendous and terrible of Canaanite religion, at least in one of its forms. You do not need to be a Christian to see that it was ethically horrible. The ancient Israelites, or some of them, saw that clearly enough. So too, Chesterton suggested, did the ancient Romans when they met the adherents of this cult in the Carthaginians (Carthage was, as we know, originally a colony from Phoenicia): 'These highly civilized people really met together to invoke the blessing of heaven on their empire by throwing hundreds of their infants into a large furnace' (*The Everlasting Man*, ch. VII). But our horror of the very idea of such a practice need not blind us to the sublime notion that could be conceived as underlying it: that nothing is too good to be sacrificed to God; that God is the supreme and absolute value to which all else must be subordinated and if need be surrendered. I am not arguing that this sublime notion was the operative factor in most of these sacrifices; but it could have been present, or could have been read into them by an observer, even though in actual fact the motive may often have been the quasi-magical one of trying to force the hand of the deity by an act of overwhelmingly powerful devotion.

Abraham, at any rate, as depicted for us in Genesis, conceives that it is God's will that he too should sacrifice his son Isaac, despite the fact that this beloved son is the child of promise, through whose progeny were to be transmitted the divine promises to Abraham's seed. So, like Paul at his conversion, Abraham sets out to obey what he takes to be a divine intimation, to prove in act that he is willing to make this sacrifice for God's sake and in his honour. No pagan Canaanite shall be able to say that he is more devoted to his Baal than Abraham is to the true God. As for God's promise for his descendants and the apparent impossibility of its fulfilment if Isaac is sacrificed, God himself would provide; nothing matters absolutely except to obey God's will here and now. But at the crucial moment, as we all remember, God intervenes and substitutes for the child an animal victim, and the promise for the future is renewed: 'In thy seed shall all the nations of the earth bless themselves, because thou hast obeyed my voice' (Gen. 22: 18). So, by a narrative far more educationally effective than a bare statement of prin-

F

ciples (it may be compared with the parables of the
Gospels), Israel was taught that God's claims are indeed
illimitable and yet not inconsistent with his attribute of
mercy or with the moral instincts which he has planted
in humanity which he 'created in his own image'.
Provided they were willing to give God all he asked,
the Israelites need not view the abominations of the
Canaanites with any sense of inferiority; human sacrifice was not the sort of thing for which God asked.
And we Christians cannot fail to reflect that, though
Isaac was not immolated, still the notion of the sacrifice
of what is most precious, the sacrifice not only of the
first-born but of the true, all-fulfilling, seed of Abraham
(Gal. 3: 16), was to find, in the working-out of divine
providence, an unforeseeable and wonderful realization
in the voluntarily accepted passion and death of Christ.
Isaac, as the Christian Fathers would have said, is a
'type' of Christ himself.

So far, however, we have not dealt with the feature
of the story in which our difficulty reaches its full
poignancy. As in some other instances in the Old Testament where a projected action is mentioned that is
repugnant to our moral ideas, the proposed sacrifice of
Isaac is made the matter of a divine command: 'Take
thy only-begotten son Isaac, whom thou lovest, and go
into the land of vision: and there thou shalt offer him
for an holocaust upon one of the mountains which I
shall show thee' (Gen. 22: 2).

How could God possibly command a ritual murder? I suggest that this question brings us to the radical truth about all revelation of God to man, namely, that it is a divine self-disclosure within human experience, and therefore subject to the limitations of the human recipient. Here the philosophical axiom holds good that 'whatever is received or known is received or known according to the measure of capacity of him who receives or knows it'. If your musical education is rudimentary, you will not 'get' as much as you might out of the greatest music—its quota of beauty is automatically reduced for you to the measure of which you are capable. The pure light of God has to be translated into human terms before it can be apprehended by man. It is only revelation in so far as it is apprehended. It is only, though truly, known as translated, and the nature and adequacy of the translation will vary with the nature and the spiritual enlightenment of the recipient of the revelation. If it is a revelation directed towards action, it will take form and shape in the conscience of the recipient and will be to some extent limited by his existing moral stature, which at the same time it may tend to enlarge. 'I have still much to say to you, but it is beyond your reach as yet' (Jn. 16: 12). It is, incidentally, this limiting factor of the human recipient that makes the gospel a 'scandal to the Jews, and to the Greeks foolishness'. Now the verdict of conscience is always the voice of God ('Our human conscience is the

Oracle of God', wrote Byron[1]), and is always to be followed without hesitation as such; it being understood, of course, that we make a proper use of our intelligence and seek the requisite information before coming to our conscientious decision. Conscience is to be followed as being the voice of God in spite of the fact that conscience often dictates a course of action which is objectively criticizable. Even in such cases the command of conscience is still the voice of God for the subject here and now, though not for others more enlightened than he, nor for himself when he has made further moral progress. Thus it may come about that a 'word of revelation' may appear to a later generation to fall short of its own moral standards.

There is, in other words, as the Church teaches, an element of imperfection in the Old Testament revelation when we consider it by itself, and not as leading men on to its further development in the gospel; 'the law', which we may take as standing for the whole Old Testament dispensation, 'had nothing in it of final achievement' (Heb. 7: 19). The Old Testament and the religion of which it is a record take on their full glory when they are seen as a preparation for something which outstrips their scope. The absolute and perfect revelation needed for its embodiment and its medium the perfect human nature and complete moral integrity

[1] The sentiment must surely antedate Byron; but I have not found an earlier expression of it.

and perfection of Our Lord himself within the company
of the new Israel. In that final revelation the Old Testament has its place, and we may well remind ourselves
that the twofold precept of charity (Thou shalt love the
Lord thy God with all thy heart . . . and thy neighbour
as thyself) is a combination of two Old Testament texts.

*Note.* The Tradition of the Pharisees.

It has been argued above that in the Judaism of the
age in which Our Lord proclaimed the gospel there was
a living 'unwritten' tradition, alongside the written
Bible, and that this unwritten tradition was itself a guide
to religious living. It may, however, be objected that
the actual word 'tradition' is found, in the Gospels, only
at Mt. 15: 2–6, and the parallel passage in Mk. 7: 3–19,
and that here tradition comes under Our Lord's strong
condemnation:

> Jesus was approached by the scribes and Pharisees from
> Jerusalem, who asked: Why is it that thy disciples violate
> the tradition of our ancestors? They do not wash their
> hands when they eat. He answered them, Why is it that
> you yourselves violate the commandment of God with
> your traditions? . . . By these traditions of yours you have
> made God's law ineffectual. You hypocrites, it was a true
> prophecy Isaias made of you when he said, This people
> does me honour with its lips, but its heart is far from me.
> Their worship of me is vain, for the doctrines they teach
> are the commandments of men. (Mt. 15: 1–9.)

This incident is clear proof that Our Lord did not teach that all that was claimed as traditional by the 'scribes and Pharisees' was either truly authoritative or laudable. In other words, this tradition was not an infallible index of divine truth or of God's will. Have we, then, any right to claim infallibility for any form of Christian tradition?

Before attempting to answer this question, it may be well to point out that the New Testament itself speaks quite differently of Christian tradition from the way in which Pharisaic tradition is condemned in the above passage: 'I must needs praise you . . . for upholding your traditions just as I handed them on to you' (1 Cor. 11: 2); 'Hold by the traditions you have learned, in word or in writing, from us' (2 Thess. 2: 14); 'We charge you . . . to have nothing to do with any brother who lives a vagabond life, contrary to the tradition which we have handed on' (ibid., 3: 6).

There are, then, traditions and traditions. There are traditions which are to be rejected as violating God's commandments. And there are traditions which are to be upheld 'just as they have been handed on to us' by God's authorized representatives.

In default of true prophets, and before the coming of Christ himself, there was no infallible teaching authority provided in the Jewish dispensation, which, unlike Christianity, looked forward in the divine plan, for a fullness which it did not yet contain and had therefore an element of provisionalness. There was no person or body of persons superior to the Pharisees who could pass judgment on the good and the bad in the Pharisaic traditions. And Christianity would be in the same case if no infallible teaching authority had been provided for it. Readers of Newman's *Essay on the Development of Doctrine* will remember that he there argued that doctrinal development in Christianity was antecedently probable and had in fact occurred; and that, this being so, it became vital to find a teaching authority, not itself subject to error, which could discriminate between healthy and corrupt developments. This authority, of course, is the body of the bishops and the successor of St. Peter. Since we depend on tradition as our link with revelation, and since in fact development of doctrine is the process in which the Church comes to a fuller understanding of the implications of her tradition (it will be remembered that I use this word to cover both written and unwritten tradition), we can apply Newman's solution to our own problem. Pre-Christian Judaism was 'open' to the reception of fresh revelation; Christianity, with its faith in the Word Incarnate, is not. The criterion of truth in Christianity is therefore not, as it could be in Judaism, the future verdict of a prophet or of the Messiah, but must be found within the given system of Christianity. It is found in the supreme teaching authority of the Church, whose function is to discriminate between genuine and corrupt tradition.

Finally, it is to be remarked that in the Gospel passage quoted above Our Lord does not condemn Pharisaic tradition as such, but only in so far as it contradicted the Scripture record of divine revelation. Our faith in the infallibility of the Church assures us that, so far as tradition receives the guarantee of the Church, it cannot contradict the Scriptures.

# CHAPTER THREE

# The Bible and Christ

IN THE course of the previous chapter we came up against the question of the truth, in the modern scientific historical sense of that word, of the Bible. We were driven to face this question, because the Christian tradition, ratified by the Church in ecumenical council, tells us that the books of the Bible are inspired by the Holy Ghost. The Holy Ghost is the spirit of truth; what the Bible tells us is therefore, it would seem, true. But our consideration of this question led us to two conclusions, each of them, at first sight, rather depressing. One was that what the Bible actually tells us is not necessarily what it seems to say on the surface. In order to put ourselves in a position to discover, with the fullest possible depth and accuracy, what the Bible is actually asserting on the deliberate authority of its inspired authors we have to undertake an extremely professional investigation of the literary conventions to which the authors severally conformed, and beyond that of the intention which governs their personal applications of the conventions. The Bible, then, is by no means a book which 'he who runs may read' with any hope of certainty in the fruit of his reading.

Secondly, we came to the conclusion that, if we wished to discover the actual facts, the literal time-and-space events, of the historical stream which contains ancient Israel, Jesus of Nazareth, and the primitive Church, we had to accept the methods and follow the processes of historical science. All such scientific criticism and scholarship is extremely tentative in its course, and is likely to give, at the best, results of very varying degrees of probability rather than certainty. You have only to survey the story of the criticism of the Book of Genesis in the last hundred years, and to appraise the present position of this criticism,[1] to realize the truth of that. In other words, there is little finality in such critical work. We shall presumably always be left by it with a central core of what it will choose to call 'assured results', surrounded by areas of diminished assurance which shade off into complete uncertainty. And even the 'assured results' of one generation of scholars seem to be liable to revision by the next generation or the one after that.

In view of this provisional nature of the findings of critical scholarship, it may be well to remind ourselves once again that God's purpose in giving us the Bible was not primarily to promote the science of history or any other natural science; the Bible has much to give

[1] Cf. U. Simon in the *Church Quarterly Review*, April-June 1958.

us, but our chief concern is with what it has to give us in the supernatural order. We may add, with reference to the question of inerrancy, with which we have been so largely concerned, and which drove us to the necessity of expert 'exegesis', that the idea of inerrancy is in itself a negative one. It only tells us what we shall not find in the Bible, namely, a full self-committal on the part of an inspired author to an assertion which is not true in the sense in which he meant it. But the doctrine of inspiration itself is not a negative but a positive doctrine. What does this doctrine positively affirm? Can we say that it affirms that Scripture is, in a true sense, a word of God to man, an utterance of the Holy Ghost? Personally, I should like to revise even that suggestion, and say that the doctrine affirms that the several books of the Bible are words of God to us, though each of them is at the same time a word of a human author or of some human authors.

Scripture is therefore something at once human and 'spiritual'. It is as a collection of human productions that it lies open to our powers of natural enquiry and criticism, and is rightly studied with the help of those powers. But St. Paul reminds us that 'the things of the spirit'—and Scripture is, as we have just said, 'not only human but spiritual'—are discerned not naturally but spiritually; they require for their understanding more than our natural powers can by themselves provide:

No one else can know God's thoughts, but the Spirit of
God. And what we have received is no spirit of worldly
wisdom; it is the Spirit that comes from God, to make us
understand God's gifts to us. . . . Mere man with his
natural gifts cannot take in the thoughts of God's Spirit;
they seem mere folly to him, and he cannot grasp them,
because they demand a scrutiny which is spiritual (1 Cor.
2: 11–14).

It follows from this that the divine meaning of
Scripture will disclose itself, after the application of such
human scholarship and criticism as we possess, to the
spiritual understanding that accompanies a devout and
believing hearing or reading of the Bible. This divine
meaning is found less by schoolroom study than by
what we may call prayerful meditation. Was not something of the same sort true about the Word Incarnate
himself? Just as the books of the Bible are books, and to
that extent like other books—like *The Tale of Two
Cities* or *The Origin of Species*—so too the Word made
flesh was a man, and to that extent like Socrates or
David Livingstone. When he went about teaching and
performing miracles, unbelievers saw with their bodily
eyes what was there to be seen by the faculty of ordinary
sight. They could construe the natural meaning of his
words, to the extent at least that they themselves had
natural intellectual acumen. But they could never, so
far as they remained unbelievers and nothing more,
penetrate beneath these outward appearances, these

phenomena of sound and sight, to the divine meaning within:

> If I talk to them in parables, it is because, though they have eyes, they cannot see, and though they have ears they cannot hear or understand. . . . But blessed are your eyes, for they have sight; blessed are your ears, for they have hearing (Mt. 13: 13–16).

In one sense, of course, the believing disciples saw and heard just what the unbelievers saw and heard; in another sense, they saw and heard, spiritually, what was hidden from the unbelievers.

In the same way, and for the same reason, the Bible, considered as words of God inspired by the Holy Ghost, will always be a 'closed book' to those who approach it in any frame of mind other than that of humble faith. It records a revelation made not to the 'wise and prudent' as such, but to God's 'little children', and 'unless we become like little children' we shall not enter into the kingdom of the Bible. Its pages can convey to the unbeliever a world of interesting information about the cultural history of antiquity and the 'natural history' of the Israelite-Christian religion and the People of God. But, so far at least as he is nothing more than an unbeliever, confined within the prison-house of his unbelief and not wishing to emerge, it will not disclose to him the wisdom and the power of God (1 Cor. 1: 24). He will be like a man listening to a performance of

Bach, but completely destitute of the very foundations
of musical appreciation. Such a man could master the
mathematical bases of the rhythm and of the interrelated notes of the music. But he could not appreciate
the musical quality of what he heard; he would be
'deaf' to it. Hearing, he would hear and not understand.

Who, then, is the devout and faithful listener *par
excellence*, to whom the books of the Old and New
Testament, as inspired words of God, are addressed?
We may suppose that they are addressed to the same
person or persons as was, or were, destined to receive
by transmission the revelation of God for whose contents we turn to their pages. Now we saw in the first
lecture that the recipient of the divine revelation was
the Chosen People of God, Israel, whether 'Old' or
'New'. The revelation under the Former Dispensation
was made to the ancient Israel, the people of the Mosaic
covenant. And in fact the Old Testament books may be
described as the ripe fruit of the age-long life of that
People of God, a life lived, so far as it was pleasing to
God, under the aegis of God's words to Moses and the
prophets. And when we turn to the New Dispensation
and the New Covenant (or Testament; the words represent the same Greek word) we again find that the
revelation is addressed to the People of God. Our Lord
made his personal appeal to the House of Israel. And
when it appeared that Jewish officialdom would not
accept his claim, he refashioned Israel, the Israel of God,

as the 'little flock' of those who did receive him. It was round their acceptance of him, round their faith in him, that he organized the body that was to transmit his message, to transmit himself, since the Word made flesh and his message were identical, to you and me in this twentieth century.

The message of the Bible, the revelation it contains, is directed not immediately to the individual Christian and his private judgment but directly to the Church, the Community of the Messiah. And since, as we have seen, it is those who have the Holy Spirit to enlighten and enable their natural faculties who alone can discern the things of the Spirit of God, we are not surprised to read in Acts that the Pentecostal Gift of the Holy Ghost was poured out upon the Church, the New Israel, the divinely fashioned collectivity of those who accept the final revelation of God.[1] The individual Christian is one who by faith and baptism has been incorporated into the Church, the Body of Christ. Only so does he too become in his own measure and by participation—or, to use the New Testament word, by communion— with her, a devout and humble believer, himself indwelt by the Holy Ghost: 'Be baptized, every one of you, in the name of Jesus Christ, to have your sins for-

---

[1] It is probable that in Acts 2: 1 the 'all' who are gathered together are not only the Twelve but the wider company referred to in 1: 15 (cf. 2: 15 'these men'). If, however, 'all' means 'all the Twelve', the Twelve represent the Church.

given; then you will receive the gift of the Holy Spirit'
(Acts 2: 38). 'You are one body, with a single Spirit'
(Eph. 4: 4). We infer that the Scriptures in their spiritual
significance are not handed over in the first instance to
the spiritual judgment of individuals. The individual
reads them, if he does so aright and with hope of
spiritual profit and learning, as a member of the Body,
sharing in the Body's mind. Ultimately, it is for the
Church, which the Holy Ghost leads 'into all truth'
(Jn. 16: 13), to discern, and to declare to her children
who are also her members, the spiritual meaning of
Scripture, its meaning for faith; to determine, for
instance, that This is my body is not a mere poetic use
of a symbol, a sort of empty parable, but a statement of
true, though mysterious, fact. Only rarely does the
Church thus settle once for all the meaning of a particular text. But she is always at work defining the
meaning of Scripture as a whole. It should perhaps be
added, since the point is sometimes misunderstood, that
what the Church does not and cannot do is to substitute
for the word of God a word of its own devising. Its
task is to present to the contemporary world, with such
explanation as the times require, the revelation that was
handed down, once for all, to the saints (Jude 3) and
has been embedded in the tradition, whether written or
unwritten. For an example of such explanation we may
take the word 'consubstantial', inserted into the Creed,
in order to assert the full godhead of Christ, by the

ecumenical Council of Nicaea in A.D. 325. This is an unscriptural word, that is to say the word itself is not found in the Bible; nor is it likely that the actual word came down by unwritten tradition from apostolic times. But by adopting it the Church has defined that its meaning was latent in the tradition from the first.

The books of the Bible, then, are each a word of God addressed to humanity as incorporated in the divinely founded universal fellowship which is called the Catholic Church. Each book has something to tell us. But if we want to sum up the message of the whole collection of books, this can be done in the single word Christ. The Old Testament Scripture prepares the way for, looks forward to, and in a sense 'prefigures' Christ, in whom, as the word of God, all its divine teaching is subsumed and raised to a higher level. The New Testament expounds Christ, the 'whole Christ' of St. Augustine's celebrated phrase; Christ in his Church, and the Church as the Body of which he is the head. In another well-known dictum St. Augustine says that the New Testament lies concealed within the Old, and the Old Testament lies disclosed in the New. If we remember that the word Testament translates a Greek word which can also be translated Covenant, and that Our Lord himself is God's new covenant with man, we can accept that statement as true. It is another way of saying, with the Epistle to the Hebrews (10: 1) that the Old Testament law is the shadow of those blessings which were

G

still to come, not the full expression of their reality.

The broad truth of the statement that Christ is the inner meaning of the Old Testament is plain enough though the full wealth of its significance is something that not all the centuries of the Church's past and future life on earth will have been too long to exploit.

The faith and religious practice of pre-Christian Israel, in the form in which they have been crystallized in the pages of the Old Testament and as they actually existed at the beginning of the Christian era, stand out as something practically unique against their background of earlier and contemporay religion, magic, astrology and philosophy. It has been argued that man's most primitive faith was a perhaps naive but yet genuine monotheism; it has been argued, and it has of course been disputed. But long before the time of Moses this pure faith, if it ever existed, had receded into the background before a proliferation of animism, fetishism, totemism, polytheistic cults, mythology and magic. There were protests against this state of things in the more advanced cultures of Persia and Greece in the last thousand years before Christ. In Persia, Zoroastrianism was a noble, if not ultimately very successful, effort to substitute, not indeed full monotheism, but at least a very lofty ethical dualism for the traditional polytheistic religion. Greek rationalism and philosophy made a similar, though not thoroughly intransigent, attempt to offer to an *élite* a purer and truer world-outlook than that of popular paganism; and in the teaching of the post-Christian philosopher Plotinus it seems to have achieved genuine monotheism. But neither of these attempts succeeded in the long run in imposing itself on a whole nation or empire, to become its corporate and traditional religion. The earlier attempt in the reign of Ikhnaton to establish strict solar 'monotheism' in Egypt lasted less than a generation before a violent reaction restored the *status quo*. We can point to such protests as the witness to the truth of man's *anima naturaliter Christiana*; but also as evidence, through their failure, of the apparently insuperable obstacles to the triumph of religious truth.

In Israel, however, as a result mainly of the work of Moses and the prophets, a pure and exalted monotheism, confident in itself and intransigent towards false religion, had, by the time of Christ, become the faith of a whole nation, with its centre in Palestine, Jerusalem, and the Temple, but with outposts throughout the Near East and the Mediterranean world at least as far afield as the city of Rome. So clearcut was the Jewish rejection of paganism that the Romans regarded the Jews as atheists, because they refused point-blank to have any truck with the gods amany who crowded the civilized pantheon.

The faith of Israel never purported to be the fruit of hard critical philosophic thinking like that of the Greek philosophers. An occasional Biblical text (there is one

in the Book of Wisdom, another in the ?pistle to the
Romans, 1:19–21, which is probably ` ase  on Wisdom
13) points to the demonstration of God's existence
which is universally available in the very fact of the
created universe. But this argument was rather a stick
with which to beat the unbelieving pagan than a ground
of faith for the Israelite believer. To the devout Israelite,
faith (a virtue about which we hear little in the Old
Testament) was grounded in God's self-revelation to his
Chosen People in saving deeds, which were the 'evidence' of his presence with them, and through divinely
inspired messengers. In other words, he was known to
the men of his choice in his redeeming activity, and the
almighty power herein disclosed presupposed, of course,
his creative activity. The atmosphere of Israelite theological thought, as also the close connection between
the idea of God and that of his actual historical people,
can be caught in the following passage:

> Here is a message from the Lord (i.e. Jahveh, the name by
> which, it was believed, God had revealed himself to his
> people) to Jacob his creature, to the Israel he fashioned:
> Do not be afraid, I have bought thee for myself, and given
> thee the name thou bearest: thou belongest to me. Pass
> through water, and I will be with thee, so that the flood
> shall not drown thee; walk amid the flames, and thou
> shalt not be burnt, the fire shall have no power to catch
> thee. I am Jahveh thy God, the Holy One of Israel, thy
> deliverer; I have bartered away Egypt to win thee,

Ethiopia and Saba for thy ransom. So prized, so honoured, so dearly loved, that I am ready to give up mankind in thy place, a world to save thee. Do not be afraid, I am with thee. . . . (Is. 44: 1–5).[1]

This notion of a loving, speaking, active, intervening God is to be contrasted with the typical Greek philosophic notion of the Unmoved Mover, which is not attracted by things inferior to himself but, according to Aristotle, attracts them as a lover is attracted (not by a lover but) by his beloved. The Unmoved Mover is a lodestar; Jahveh is a betrayed husband who goes to seek and recover the love of Israel his wife (Hos. 2: 14).

Ethical monotheism, with the idea of the Covenant People, is the supreme achievement of the Israelite-Jewish faith. It was a truth to which the Jews had attained by a path other than that of critical philosophic thinking. Nevertheless, it is the doctrine in which the most sincere and exigent philosophic thinking itself culminates—though it had to wait till the thirteenth century after Christ for its at all adequate philosophic

[1] Thus, the God who has all the nations as his possession is ready to purchase his special ownership of Israel at the cost of all the other nations. Later, Jews would say that it was on account of the Chosen People that the world was created (Assumption of Moses 1: 12). As we have seen, for Christianity the Church is the New Israel, and it is interesting to find this Jewish notion applied to the Church in the second-century Shepherd of Hermas: 'The Church . . . was created the first of all things . . . and for her sake the world was established' (4: 1).

grounding and exposition. If there is any validity in the concept of moral miracle, the faith of ancient Israel and its effects in practice may surely claim to be an example of such. How was it that, while elsewhere the impulse towards an elevated moral monotheism proved so abortive, the Israelites or Jews, without appeal to philosophy, brought it to triumphal development as their national faith, thus paving the way for, and eventually (through the mediation of the Christian Church) stimulating the much later philosophical achievement? Certainly, anyone who thinks that such monotheism is the true answer to man's deepest questionings, and who wonders whether God has ever stretched out a hand or uttered a summons to mankind from behind the veil of creatures that hides him, cannot fail to find his attention irresistibly drawn to this small and in some ways (to us) unattractive people and to the literature in which their religious traditions are embodied.[1]

One of the highest points, perhaps the highest, in this literature, is reached in the latter part of the Book of Isaias (specially chapters 40–55). In this section of the book, from which I have just quoted, ethical monotheism makes its most sublime self-affirmation over

[1] That God will, in fact, have thus 'stretched out his hand' is argued forcibly by Bernard Lonergan in *Insight*, ch. XX, e.g.: 'There is a problem of evil, for besides man there is also God. . . . Because God is omniscient, he knows man's plight. Because he is omnipotent, he can remedy it. Because he is good, he wills to do so,' p. 694.

against both the polytheism of paganism and the national disappointments of the Jews. The truth of God's choice of Israel is reasserted in spite of everything which seems to contradict it. But the people's vocation is represented as being not simply for their own benefit but as involving a witness for God and a mission of enlightenment, to be undertaken by them or on their behalf, and directed to mankind at large. This tremendous idea seems to be closely connected with that of the Suffering Servant of the Lord in these same chapters, a figure of prophecy in which Christianity has from the first[1] seen an adumbration of Jesus Christ:

> (The Servant is speaking). And now saith the Lord, that formed me from the womb to be his servant, that I may bring back Jacob unto him, and Israel will be gathered together. . . . 'It is a small thing that thou shouldest be my servant to raise up the tribes of Jacob, and to convert the dregs of Israel. Behold, I have given thee to be the light of the Gentiles, that thou mayest be my salvation even to the farthest part of the earth.' (Is. 49: 5 f.)

It is a fact that, broadly speaking, Israel's missionary work to the world in general has, since the beginning of the Christian era, been carried into effect mainly by the Church which Christ founded, and by the other Christian bodies which, at various times down the centuries, have broken away from the Church, but carried

[1] Cf., for instance, Acts 8: 27–39.

with them something of her traditions and inspiration.[1]
For the historian, then, there is a true sense in which the
Old Testament finds its continuation in the new dispen-
sation; its continuation and its universal application.
And the message of the new dispensation, as of the New
Testament books in which that message attained an
early crystallization, is Christ himself.

We have seen that the central point of Christian
belief is that Christ is God's supreme self-revelation and
summons to man; he is the word of God incarnate.
And on the other hand, as we have seen, the books of
the Bible, whether of the Old or the New Testament,
are, according to the Church's teaching, words of God
to us. But if Christ is the sum and substance of God's
self-disclosure, these Biblical words of God must be,
directly or indirectly, words about, or words pointing
to, Christ. It is obvious that Christ is the focal-point
and the meaning of the New Testament books. And if
Christ, his gospel, and the Church his body, are the
divinely intended consummation of the revelation and
promises to ancient Israel, if these are the things which
prophets and just men desired to see and hear (Mt. 13:
17), yet saw and heard not except in mysterious anticipa-
tion and prefigurement, then it follows that Christ is

---

[1] Christians and Jews must not forget that a large part of humanity
owes its monotheistic faith immediately to Islam. I have suggested, in
the first of these lectures, that Islam can be regarded, historically, as a
sort of heretical by-product of the Jewish-Christian tradition.

also the goal and meaning of the Old Testament books. We are back again at St. Augustine's saying: The New Testament lies hidden in the Old, the Old Testament has its meaning disclosed in the New.

Now it may be asked: Since in Christ we have the substance of what ancient Israel hoped for and what the Old Testament only foreshadows, why should we bother ourselves with the Old Testament, its shadows and prefigurements at all—especially since, as George V said and we have virtually admitted, this wonderful book contains some very queer things? I tried to deal with some of these queer things in the previous lecture, reminding you that ancient Israel's education in the things of God and his will was a very long and gradual thing. Still, why should we ponder on the rudimentary lessons of that distant past, when we have Christ himself, the image of God the invisible (Col. 1: 15), Christ in whom are all the treasures of wisdom and knowledge (ibid., 2: 3)?

Well, yes, we have Christ. Do we try to make him live for our imagination and our understanding as a real, divine but very human, personal reality—someone whom we can love not as an abstract formula of perfection but as an actual, vivid, friend? We have him in our hearts by faith and baptism and Holy Communion; we have him in the mystery of the presence of the Tabernacle. Yes; but as what? As God with us (but he is also man). But what is God to us? God the invisible,

God the incomprehensible, God whom we do not know and cannot know as a friend unless he chooses to reveal himself. And it is the divine but also human Son of Mary, it is Jesus of Nazareth, who is the revelation of God. He that has seen me has seen the Father (Jn. 14: 9). How can we know the human Jesus who is God self-revealed? From *The Imitation of Christ*, the hymns of St. Bernard and Faber, the statues and pictures in our churches and our homes? All these may help. But surely the best, the most direct, the most fully authorized source is the inspired pages of the New Testament and in particular of the Gospels. There, if anywhere, we may hope to discover, by devout and intelligent reading, the materials out of which grace will build up for us the living personality of our Saviour.

But now, how are we to understand the New Testament and the Gospels? To understand a historical personage—which is what the Son of God has willed to become for us—you have to see him in his historical setting. In the incarnation the Word of God did not merely assume a human nature. He entered the time process, he accepted a particular human environment, he 'subjected himself' to a particular set of human historical conditions. He was the son of Mary, the foster-child of Joseph the carpenter; he was the child who 'could not' (as you might say) drag himself away from the fascination of the Temple which summed up all Israel's faith and hope, and from the doctors of the Law who embodied Israel's traditional lore and wisdom. He was the man who submitted to baptism by John; the friend of Peter and of the Twelve (Judas included); he who was sent to 'the lost sheep of the house of Israel' and taught them in terminology which their traditional culture would help them to understand. Their traditional culture? But it was the tradition in which he himself had grown up. As the child Jesus advanced in wisdom and in stature it was on the faith and piety of ancient Israel that his human mind was nourished, as this faith and piety were taught to him at his Mother's knee and in the rabbinic town school, as the record of them were in due course read by himself in the Sacred Books. It was in the pages of the Old Testament that, as man, he read his own Messianic vocation; and it was in Old Testament forms and figures that he clothed it for himself and others. We cannot adequately understand him or his words or even his miracles apart from this particular human context in which he humanly came to understand himself; and that is surely a great reason for studying and valuing the Old Testament in which all that he has to tell us is steeped. The human context of Jesus's life included a social and revelational religion, with institutional, mystical and (in a non-Greek sense) intellectual elements. Characteristic among its embodiments were the Mosaic Law, the worship of the Temple with its sacrifice and psalmody, the wisdom of its doctors and sages, the insight of its prophets, and the Messianic ideas which had grown up round the notions of an ideal Davidic king, which he himself, it may be suggested, synthesized with the figures of the Suffering Servant and of the Danielic one like unto a son of man (cf. Dan. 7). All this not only fed and gave form to his personal human piety (and he is the model of our own devotion); it was, in substance, both endorsed by him as valid for its own epoch, and transcended in the religious manifold-in-unity which he established—somewhat in the way in which life accepts and transmutes inorganic matter. In him the pre-Christian tradition of Israel and the specifically Christian tradition find their unity, each gaining its full meaning through interrelation with the other. So, if we really want to know him, God made man, we must pay attention to both the New Testament and the Old.

The Church herself sets us an example in this matter. Week by week we come together, at her invitation 'on the first day of the week' (cf. Acts 20: 7) to 'do in Christ's remembrance' what he did at the Last Supper. The chant with which this act of corporate worship is beautified is set to words taken as a rule from the Bible, either Old or New Testament. The Scripture read before the Gospel is usually from one of the New Testament Epistles, but sometimes from the Old Testament. And when we pass on to the Great Prayer, or Canon of the Mass, in which the sacrifice is offered, we are not only following in the train of a Jewish pattern of 'thanksgiving' or 'blessing of God', introduced by what was perhaps a Jewish pattern of versicle and response ('Let us give thanks . . .', 'It is meet and right so to do'), but we are still drawing on the Old Testament in the prayer itself for the Sanctus, Hosanna (note the Jewish word) *in excelsis, Sacrificium laudis, Reddunt vota sua, Patriarchae nostri* (our patriarch!) Abraham, Melchizedech; and in true Jewish fashion, having begun by acknowledging our duty to 'thank God' (probably originally this meant to 'bless' him) we conclude by ascribing to him 'all honour and glory'. Our debt to the Old Testament, and therefore to ancient Israel, comes out with special clearness in the new liturgy of the Easter Vigil, which sets the great act of our redemption in a framework of creation and providence seen through Old Testament eyes. At the very heart of the Mass, when we actually represent to God what Our Lord did at the Last Supper and commanded us to continue, it is probable that we are employing a Jewish mode of worship transformed to be the sacrament of a new covenant which can only be understood in the light of the old covenant. How extremely grateful ought we to be to our Israelite and Jewish forefathers in the faith. How we ought to feel that gratitude going out from within us towards every Jew with whom we come in contact. With what gratitude, charity and respect ought we not to pray for the Jews that they may be brought to recognize with us that, great as was their gift of the Old

Testament to us, the gift they gave us in Jesus Christ
was far greater, and was and is intended for them no less
than for us:

> They are Israelites, adopted as God's sons; the visible
> presence, and the covenant, and the giving of the law, and
> the Temple worship, and the promises, are their inheritance;
> the patriarchs belong to them, and theirs is the human
> stock from which Christ came, who is supreme over all
> things (Rom. 9: 4 f.).

The public devotion of the Church and the private
devotion of her children both look back, or should do
so, to the New and Old Testaments. What of theology?
All Christian theology goes back continually to the
Bible, because dogmatic theology is simply the attempt
to express, in scientific thought and language, to
develop, and to relate to other branches of knowledge,
the contents of the revelation of which tradition, written
or unwritten, is the deposit. Scripture and the unwritten
deposit, Scripture and the daily teachings and well-
stored mind of the contemporary Church, are the living
sources, the well-head, the *fons et origo*, upon which
theology draws. They are sources which live in and by
the life of the Holy Spirit in the Church. The last thirty
years or so, and especially, for Catholics, the last twenty
years, have witnessed an immense reinvigoration of
New Testament study and appreciation. This revival
owes much of its vigour to a renewed and sustained

attempt to see the New Testament and the primitive Church in the light thrown upon them by their Old Testament presuppositions. And on the other hand this revival is shedding its own light on, and will in due course gives its own stimulus to, dogmatic theology.

Historically speaking, theology has practically grown out of the study of Scripture. Perhaps the greatest creator of New Testament thought in the first three Christian centuries (excepting of course the New Testament writers themselves) was the famous Egyptian scholar named Origen. He wrote in Greek; or rather, he seems to have dictated in Greek, in the days of his great productivity, to one or other of his six shorthand secretaries. The influence of his work pervades wide areas of subsequent theological thought in Greek-speaking Christendom, and was to some extent transmitted to the West in translation and through the works of St. Ambrose. A large part of his writings consisted in commentaries, sermons, or lectures on the Scriptures; and it is characteristic of him that he finds Christ in Old and New Testaments alike—sometimes by dint of an allegorical or typological exegesis that is very uncongenial to us! The greatest theologian among the Western Fathers was St. Augustine, and he too was deep in the Scriptures, and has left us what are in effect commentaries on the Psalms and on St. John's Gospel. I need only mention St. Jerome, because he was a Biblical scholar rather than a theologian, and the

Western Church has used his Latin translation of the
Scriptures for centuries.

What is perhaps not so generally recognized is that
when, in the Middle Ages, that new approach of systematic thought, based partly on natural theology,
began to be made to Christian truth which we call
scholastic theology, once again it was to the Bible above
all (along with the liturgy and the witness of the Fathers)
that the scholastics turned as to the source or spring
from which to draw that content of revelation which
they then sought to understand more deeply by apply-
ing to it the principles of logical thinking. There is a
tendency in some quarters today to depreciate logical
thinking, even, or especially, when the matter at issue
is religious truth. This sometimes leads people to condemn scholasticism as a rationalization of the gospel, if
not also to regret the earlier work of the patristic age in
adapting the gospel to the framework of Greek thought.
But what criterion have you to distinguish religious, or
any other sort of, truth from falsehood if you give up
logic? The Church has the task of proclaiming and
recommending the gospel to the world, and whether in
the age of Origen and Augustine, in that of Thomas
Aquinas, or today it has to try to show men that in
accepting her message they will not be doing violence
to the intellect, the faculty of truth which nature, that
is to say God the creator of nature, has planted in them.
Of course the so-called logical thinker may misuse his

natural gift; he may atrophy his sense of mystery and deny to mystery itself its rightful place. But the abuse of a faculty does not deprive it of its proper rights. It is also true that in the process of translating Christianity into the categories of Greece, which we have ourselves inherited, it is possible to lose sight of some elements of the total tradition. The Greek and Latin Fathers of the Church lacked the modern Biblical scholar's awareness of the nature of the Israelite or Jewish presuppositions of Biblical language and thought, and their exegesis of Scripture was often, to our way of thinking, wildly at fault. But the Holy Ghost has saved the Church, and will always save her, from finally committing herself and her children to error, and the Bible is always there to become the source of theological revival.

The study of the Bible, whether we mean the critical and exegetical work of the historian and the scholar, or the prayerful meditation of the individual believing Christian, is never complete and will never be completed. Nor can it be expected to give at any time more than a modicum of 'assured results'. Certainty belongs to the articles of the faith, in defining which the Church relies on divine guidance in her interpretation of tradition, especially the written tradition of the Bible. Certainty also belongs to the inferences which reason necessarily draws from these articles in dogmatic theology. All Bible study, if it is not to go astray, must in the end conform itself to the limits of interpretation

H

laid down by these two connected sources of certainty. But in the meantime, and within the limits of its own operations, it is of the essence of the critical method that it proceeds by trial and error, by hypothesis and revision of hypotheses. We must not be disturbed if at any particular moment the provisional findings of criticism and scholarship do not entirely coincide with the requirements of the faith and of dogmatic theology. If criticism and scholarship are not allowed to make their mistakes they will not, in the long run, be able to supply their positive results and enriching insights for the fecundation of dogmatic theology.

The several books of the Bible have been described, in the course of these lectures, as words of God. It has also been pointed out that the Word of God is the Son of God incarnate, Jesus Christ. It is also important to remember that the Church's basic task is not precisely to preach the many partial words of God, but to preach and to convey to men Christ himself, the Word made flesh. But the Church conveys Christ to men not simply by proclaiming and expounding the words of Scripture, but by its whole sacramental ministry and by its liturgy. Once we realize this very obvious truth, we see that it can be misleading to speak of the clergy as 'ministers of the word and the sacraments'; because this might suggest that it is not the Word who is ministered to us in the sacraments—that he is only ministered to us in the proclamation and exposition of Scripture. The real distinction, if one is to be made, is between the spoken or written word and what we may call the sacramental word. That distinction is broadly illustrated in the Mass, which is divided into two parts, the so-called Mass of the catechumens (up to the end of the Gospel), and the Mass of the faithful in which the sacramental sacrifice is offered and the sacrificial sacrament received. About the Mass of the catechumens, two points are of interest. First, it seems to be a transference to the worship of the Church of the old Synagogue services of pre-Christian Judaism. But then, is not the sacrifice of the Mass, in the prayer of Eucharist or Blessing, a transference and transposition, an elevation, of a Jewish ceremony, whether we think of this as a Passover or as a brother-hood meal? Secondly, how interesting it is to see, in the ceremonies which accompany the reading of the Gospel at High Mass, the esteem which the Church has for the written word of God. The Church's ceremonies are meaningful gestures; they are the language of action. In some streams of Protestant tradition there has been a great suspicion of 'rites and ceremonies'. But, despite the danger of exaggerated 'ritualism', I cannot think that this suspicion is entirely justifiable. Language itself is a set of meaningful audible or legible signs; it is a way of communicating one's meaning. There are other ways of doing the same thing. When a man takes off his hat to a lady, he is expressing a meaning of courtesy not by word but by act; he is making use of what we may call a ceremony of polite society. So too, when a Catholic of the Latin rite genuflects to the Blessed Sacrament, or a Catholic of a different age or rite bows to It, he is making a meaningful gesture. I can understand a Protestant objecting to this gesture as an act of idolatry; but granted the Catholic faith in the Real Presence, I cannot see why in principle the gesture is objectionable because it is a gesture. We read in the Apocalypse that when the four living figures, in the vision of heaven, gave glory to God, 'the twenty-four elders fell down in worship . . . and threw down their crowns before the throne, crying out, Thou, our Lord God, claimest as thy due glory and honour and power' (4: 10 f.). Obviously, this is symbolic language; but is it not equally obvious that the writer thinks it entirely appropriate that creatures of flesh and blood should express their worship by the very posture of their bodies, and by such significant acts as 'throwing down their crowns'? Correlation of mind and body is not a bad educational principle.

To return to the ceremonies at the reading of the Gospel. We see the deacon at High Mass laying the book of the Gospels on the consecrated altar, where later on the priest will lay the sacrament of Our Lord's body. We watch him praying that God would cleanse his heart and lips as he cleansed the lips of the Israelite prophet Isaias with a live coal, so that he may fitly proclaim God's holy Gospel—Isaias's lips were cleansed that he might be the mouthpiece of the word of God;

and in proclaiming the Gospel the deacon, in his turn, will be proclaiming God's word. Having obtained a blessing from the priest, the deacon then goes in procession, accompanied by lights and incense (except at a Requiem Mass), to the place where the Gospel is to be sung (this place should, for preference, be an ambo facing the people). He prays that God may be 'with' his hearers, and they make a similar prayer for him; ultimately, we remember, the word of God is the word uttered by the Holy Spirit to souls enlightened by the same Holy Spirit. And he incenses the book three times, and afterwards it is kissed reverently by the priest. These elaborate ceremonies show clearly that not only does the priest give Christ sacramentally, but the deacon is conceived as giving Christ the Word to the congregation. Christ comes to the mind of the Christian in order to prepare him for his coming to his heart.

It is time to draw towards a close. Let me then remind you of some of the ground we have tried to cover in these pages.

We began by taking a look at Christianity as though from the outside. It is one (we should say the most important, and its adherents are certainly the most numerous) of the three great faiths which base their teaching on an alleged self-revelation of God. Judaism, Islam and Christianity alike point back to the pre-Christian history of the nation of Israel as the context

of at least the early stages of this process of revelation.
But Christianity maintains that all the Old Testament
revelation was but preparation for and partial prefigurement of the final and supreme revelation of God
in the incarnation of the Second Person of the holy
Trinity.

Revelation by incarnation is essentially public revelation as distinct from private. That is to say it is addressed
to man not just as one separate and independent individual but to man in a social existence. Such revelation recognizes, so to speak, the fact that we are social
beings, interdependent, finding the full enrichment of
our personalities in the privileges and responsibilities of
social life. And if such a revelation was the one final
revelation, intended, as Christianity says it was, for all
mankind and all ages, then the content of the revelation
has got to be handed down and carried abroad by a
process which we have called tradition in the wide
sense; we have used this word tradition to cover both
written documents and all other, including oral, modes
of transmission.

Just as the Old Testament revelations were given to a
collectivity, to the Israelite-Jewish nation conceived as
the Chosen People of God, so too the final revelation,
the Word made flesh, was given to a collectivity: to the
People of God refashioned on a new basis, the basis,
that is to say, of faith in Christ's claims. It was originally
given to this 'little flock of the Christ', to this 'Israel

according to the Spirit', by unwritten communication, in the actual daily life of the group of human beings of which Jesus was the leader and the centre. And by such unwritten communication it continued, in large measure, to be conveyed by the Church in the earliest period of its existence after the first Christian Pentecost. Gradually, over a period of seventy years or more, the books of the New Testament came to be written by members of the Church in response to the Church's needs.

It is the abiding conviction and teaching of the Church that these documents are inspired by the Holy Ghost. They crystallize a more or less complete cross-section of the unwritten tradition of the Church; and this unwritten tradition, this voice of the living Church, continued side by side with the now written tradition. A Catholic is at liberty to hold that the written tradition is not in fact complete, but that elements of the total original tradition have survived outside the covers of the New Testament. But in any case, ever since the New Testament books began to circulate in the first-century Church, there has been a sort of cross-fecundation going on between the written and the unwritten streams of tradition; the unwritten tradition (the current teaching of the Church's living voice) has nourished itself upon the written word; and the written word has been understood and interpreted in the light of the unwritten tradition. All words, written or unwritten, are

significant signs, and they depend for their meaning on
the collective mind from which and to which they are
spoken.

Inspiration means, we have suggested, that God
declares his mind or meaning to us in the scriptural
expression of the human minds of the inspired authors.
What God tells us is true, but we can only approach to
a delimitation of what God is telling us in Scripture by
entering into the minds of the human authors of its
books; and this presupposes that we appreciate the
literary conventions to which they conformed. Clearly,
what God is telling us is not precisely scientific or
critico-historical truth; he was not concerned to satisfy
our idle curiosity or to short-circuit the natural func-
tions of our human intellect. The truth he is telling us
is truth of salvation. If we want to extract from the
Biblical documents the sort of truth that scientific historians search after, we must turn to the scientific
historians themselves, hand the documents over to
them, and listen to what they will have to tell us—
always remembering that the verdicts of scientific history can be taken with a grain of salt, and will in any
case be liable to revision or even destruction by their
own creators or by the next generation of critics.

The truth of science is sought after by the natural
human reason. But the saving truth which God wills to
tell us through inspired Scripture, requires in the reader
who seeks and is to find it an illumination of the Holy

Ghost himself. In thy light we shall see light. The reader for whom the Bible is intended is in the first instance the Catholic Church herself, indwelt by the Holy Ghost; and secondly it is the individual baptized believer considered as a member of her body and as sharing in her mind, which is the mind of Christ her head.

Christ is the word of God to men, not simply in his verbal teaching, partially preserved for us in the pages of the New Testament, but in his whole impact on history, an impact which created and endowed the Church and entrusted to it the sacraments, and above all baptism and the Eucharist. The Church transmits this word of God to us by these sacramental means, not only by her preaching.

We read the Bible, both Old and New Testaments, in order that Christ may not be just an empty word in our minds, or the shorthand sign of a dogmatic formula, but a personal, loving and lovable reality, the entrancing image of God who in his own nature is invisible and inconceivable. We read it also as theologians, especially the New Testament; because the New Testament books are a very early precipitate of Christian thought and tradition, and an inspired one; as such they have a normative value for our theological speculations and provide these with many of their starting points. The Church cannot evolve doctrine *a priori* out of its innate consciousness. Doctrine is tradition intellectually grasped and articulated. Tradition itself is both preserved and investigated by ordinary human means under a guidance which is ultimately divine. But perhaps above all we read the Bible, and the Church reads it to us in her liturgy and offices, in order that we may be the better prepared to receive him who is the Word in human nature, in the sacrament of his body and blood, and there may treat with him as friends treating with our divine friend.

There is, so it seems to me, a special reason why we should return to the Scriptures with a fullness and vigour of purpose not common among us Catholics since the sad days of the Reformation period. The world is waiting for the voice of God. His message is the answer to that ultimate question which confronts each one of us in his personal life, and confronts too all our civilizations. The Catholic Church is commissioned by God to proclaim that word to mankind and every man. But there are those outside the Catholic unity who have preserved in various measures both God's words and the veneration in which they ought to be held. The non-Catholic Christians of the West, the Orthodox Eastern churches, the Copts and Nestorians—all these are with us over against the unbelieving world. But so too in their degree are the Jews and the Mohammedans, who share the Old Testament with us. The witness to God of all these bodies and separated streams of tradition is gravely prejudiced by the lack of unity amongst them and their separation from us. Cannot we join with Mohammedans and Jews in the study and meditation of the Old Testament, our common treasure? Cannot we trace with them the story of God's dealings with his Chosen People in pre-Christian days? May we not hope that in the course of such study they, like us, may come to see that neither God's promise to Israel nor the People's hope has been without fulfilment? And nearer home, cannot we join also with our separated Christian brethren in a common study not only of the Old Testament but of the New, knowing that what we all seek is the Word made flesh, but finding, on our journey to him, the Church he founded, that Messianic fellowship or community which, because of his promises, we know exists in the world today, and which, because it is a fellowship, is necessarily a single communion of believers sharing an undiminished, unmutilated, tradition, but a tradition of which we have never yet exhausted the meaning, because in the last resort its meaning is Christ who is the inexhaustible, limitless, God for whom all men, consciously or unconsciously, are thirsting? O God, thou art my God: how eager my quest for thee, body athirst and soul longing for thee, like some parched wilderness, where stream is none! (Ps. 62: 2). No lamp like thy word to guide my feet, to show light on my path (ibid., 118: 105).

# About This Book

This book is part of a series we call ARKive Editions: exact photographic reproductions of books published in previous decades or centuries. In them, you find undiluted by modern notions or passing fads the words and ideas of good and thoughtful souls who preceded us in this life.

In this, there is great value: it helps free us from the myopia that afflicts souls drowning in the words and images flooding forth from our modern media, with its attention focused so intently on that which is new and popular today.

Our age is less than perfect and ARKive Editions help us see that, enabling us to measure our own day by the often better standards of other times and places.

At the same time, previous ages and other cultures had their faults: and even in good books from earlier times we often find language, ideas, or values that were once deemed acceptable even by honorable souls, but are now seen clearly to be wrong.

We exclude from ARKive Editions books that have in them as significant themes ideas that are wrong. When, however, books that are overwhelmingly good are tainted by unfortunate peripheral remarks or occasional wrongheaded judgments, we have chosen to publish them intact. For we judge that the good to be done by such books far outweighs the harm done by occasional remarks which good men and women these days can (and should) dismiss as the unfortunate products of an age as flawed as our own, albeit in different ways.

If you disagree with our judgment, please understand, nonetheless, that we have sought to act in goodwill. Let your disagreement be an occasion for you to pray that our generation will soon come to see our own errors as clearly as we see the errors of earlier times; and then turn your attention back to the true riches that are to be found in each of our ARKive Editions, presented here exactly as they appeared to readers in earlier times.

# An Invitation

Reader, the book that you hold in your hands was published by Sophia Institute Press.

Sophia Institute seeks to restore man's knowledge of eternal truth, including man's knowledge of his own nature, his relation to other persons, and his relation to God.

Our press fulfills this mission by offering translations, reprints, and new publications. We offer scholarly as well as popular publications; there are works of fiction along with books that draw from all the arts and sciences of our civilization. These books afford readers a rich source of the enduring wisdom of mankind.

Sophia Institute Press is the publishing arm of the Thomas More College of Liberal Arts and Holy Spirit College. Both colleges are dedicated to providing university-level education in the Western tradition under the guiding light of Catholic teaching.

If you know a young person who might be interested in the ideas found in this book, share it. If you know a young person seeking a college that takes seriously the adventure of learning and the quest for truth, bring our institutions to his attention.

www.SophiaInstitute.com
www.ThomasMoreCollege.edu
www.HolySpiritCollege.org

## SOPHIA INSTITUTE PRESS

THE PUBLISHING DIVISION OF